SOUTHERN LITERARY STUDIES

Louis D. Rubin, Jr., Editor

WELCOME TO OUR CITY

WELCOME TO OUR CITY

A PLAY IN TEN SCENES BY

THOMAS WOLFE

EDITED, WITH AN INTRODUCTION,

BY RICHARD S. KENNEDY

LOUISIANA STATE UNIVERSITY PRESS

BATON ROUGE AND LONDON

This version of the play is the Harvard 47 Workshop
production script of 1923, published by permission
of the Houghton Library, Harvard University.

Also, acknowledgment is made to the University of
North Carolina Library for permission to print the
two critiques from the Wolfe Papers in the North
Carolina Collection.

Designer: Albert Crochet
Typeface: Linotron Palatino
Typesetter: G&S Typesetters, Inc.
Printer: Thomson-Shore, Inc.
Binder: John H. Dekker & Sons, Inc.

LIBRARY OF CONGRESS CATALOGING IN PUBLICATION DATA

Wolfe, Thomas, 1900–1938.
    Welcome to our city.

    (Southern literary studies)
    I. Kennedy, Richard S.   II. Title.   III. Series.
PS3545.O337W49   1983   813'.52   82-20838
ISBN 0-8071-1085-X

In memory of Paschal Reeves—
Wolfe scholar, critic, and editor

CONTENTS

A NOTE ON THE TEXT

There are a number of versions of *Welcome to Our City* in the Thomas Wolfe Collection of William B. Wisdom in the Houghton Library at Harvard. The earliest one, entitled "Niggertown," written in the autumn of 1922, survives in manuscript drafts of various scenes. Wolfe read this version to the members of George Pierce Baker's playwriting class, English 47, on January 16, 1923. One of the later typescript versions, which I will call Text A, was created for a working script when the play was produced by the 47 Workshop at Agassiz House Theater, May 11 and 12, 1923. Wolfe chose the new title, "Welcome to Our City," while the play was in rehearsal.

Wolfe's later revision and expansion of the play exists in two typescript forms: Text B, given to the Houghton Library by Aline Bernstein, has a few corrections in Wolfe's hand; and Text C (two copies), is a carbon of Text B but without Wolfe's corrections.

The present published version is based on Text A. Wolfe made a great many revisions and deletions throughout the script, especially in Scene 6. Scene 10, however, shows both notes by Professor Baker, who directed the Harvard production, and heavy cutting by Wolfe for changes that make the conclusion dramatically more effective but ones that Wolfe, no doubt, objected strongly to making.

Scenes 1 and 9 are missing from Text A. For Scene 1, I have used the Text B version, which is very similar to the autograph manuscript but has dialogue that Wolfe supplied, probably, for the Harvard production, although the characters were not named. For Scene 9, of which only one page survives, I have again used Text B. But guided by the early manuscript drafts and by interviews with W. Northrop Morse, who played the part of Mayor Sinclair, and Donald Keyes, who played the part of Colonel Grimes, I have edited the material to conform to Text A, although I strongly suspect that the description of the absurd experiment with black and white guinea pigs was dropped during rehearsal (perhaps one of those times when, as one actor reported, Wolfe gave a cry of anguish and hurriedly left the rehearsal hall). All things considered, I have assembled what seems to me the closest approximation that could be made to the production script of 1923, except for three restored lines that I judge were deleted not to improve the dramatic effect but to spare the sensibilities of the Cambridge audience, which were easily jarred by sexual references.

Readers who wish to see Wolfe's expanded, and to my mind dramatically inferior, version of *Welcome to Our City*—that is, Text B—will find Edward Aswell's abridgment of it published in *Esquire*, October, 1957, pp. 58–84. A complete version is available on microfilm from the University of North Carolina at Greensboro in Phyllis Huffman's Ph.D. dissertation, "An Edition of Thomas Wolfe's *Welcome to Our City*."

WELCOME TO OUR CITY

AGASSIZ HOUSE THEATRE

MAY 11 and 12, 1923

THE 47 WORKSHOP

PRESENTS

WELCOME TO OUR CITY

A PLAY IN TEN SCENES

BY

THOMAS CLAYTON WOLFE

Characters

BAPTIST MINISTER	Mr. Wilbur D. Dunkel
HELEN NEELY	Miss Maryalice Secoy
DAN	Mr. Grant Code
MR. JORDAN	Mr. Bates
BAILEY	Mr. R. P. Bond
SORRELL	Mr. Marvin T. Herrick
OLD SORRELL	Mr. Goodnow
UNCLE AMOS	Mr. Masten
RUTLEDGE	Mr. Cecil Rollins
LEE	Mr. John D. Lodge
MR. McINTYRE	Mr. Richard Aldrich
JOHNSON	Mr. Bushnell
HUTCHINGS	Mr. Goodnow
GOVERNOR CARR	Mr. Pearson
BULL	Mr. W. E. Stilwell, Jr.
DOGGY	Mr. P. W. Holmes
MARY TODD	Miss Googins
MRS. WHEELER	Miss Morris
ANNIE	Miss Sands
MRS. RUTLEDGE	Miss Halman
PICKENS GAFFNEY	Mr. Philip Rice
SLEW-FOOT	Mr. W. E. Stilwell, Jr.
SAM TIPTON	Mr. Grant Code
WHITE CHAUFFEUR	Mr. Robert Leven
SYKES	Mr. W. L. Smyser
REVEREND MR. SMALLWOOD	Mr. Wilbur D. Dunkel
SINCLAIR, THE MAYOR	Mr. W. T. Morse
TYSON, THE BANKER	Mr. Robert Leven
WEBSTER, THE PUBLISHER	Mr. P. W. Holmes
COLONEL GRIMES	Mr. Donald W. Keyes
TOUGH SERGEANT	Mr. Richard Aldrich
GUARDSMAN	Mr. Bates

Negroes

Mr. W. Cromwell	Mr. E. M. Littell	Mr. T. Wagner
Mr. E. H. Dewey	Mr. E. Mills	Mr. M. Walker
Mr. B. F. Everett	Mr. O. McConnell	Mr. Y. Wendell
Mr. A. Finney	Mr. J. Shute	Mr. H. J. Williams
Mr. T. La Farge	Mr. C. M. Smart	Mr. B. P. Wilson
Mr. W. E. Harris	Mr. W. S. Wilson	

Negro Girls

Miss B. Fitz Miss L. Jordan Miss D. Leadbetter Miss A. Macready

Playbill for the original performance at Harvard

SCENE	I.	A Street in Niggertown.
"	II.	The Office of The Altamont Development Company 8.30 in the morning.
"	III.	The same, one hour later.
"	IV.	A Lounge and Smoking Room at the Altamont Country Club on a night two weeks later.
"	V.	A Room in the home of the negro Johnson, the same night.
"	VI.	The Library of Rutledge, the same night.
"	VII.	A Bedroom Suite at the Altamont Inn, midnight.
"	VIII.	Same as Scene I — the next morning.
"	IX.	Same as Scenes II and III — late afternoon one week later.
"	X.	Interior of the Shoe Repair-Shop of Amos Todd—same afternoon.

The set for this play was designed and painted by Mr. John McAndrew.

Mr. Code's dance arranged by Prof. Charles D. Leslie.

THE 47 WORKSHOP
THE COMPANY

MISS MARGUERITE BARR	MR. ROBERT T. BUSHNELL
MISS RUTH B. DELANO	MR. HENRY F. CARLTON
MISS DOROTHY GOOGINS	MR. NORMAN B. CLARK
MISS DORIS F. HALMAN	MR. JOSEPH CURTIN
MISS LILLIAN R. HARTIGAN	MR. EDWARD P. GOODNOW
MISS BETTY LA MONT	MR. CHARLES S. HOWARD
MISS KATHLEEN MIDDLETON	MR. WILLIAM F. MANLEY
MISS ANGELA MORRIS	MR. STEWART MASTEN
MISS EDITH COBURN NOYES	MR. OVIATT MCCONNELL
MISS DOROTHY SANDS	MR. F. C. PACKARD, Jr.
MR. HAROLD BATES	MR. LEON M PEARSON
MR. ROYAL BEAL	MR. CECIL ROLLINS ✝
MR. JOHN MASON BROWN	MR. CONRAD SALINGER
MR. JAMES W. D. SEYMOUR	

"Each year the company shall be made up of members who have acted in the preceding season and any persons who have done distinguished work in at least two performances. Past members may be reinstated by acting in any production." Voted by the Executive Committee, November 3, 1921.

THE ARTISTIC AND PRODUCING FORCE

MR. PHILIP BARBER	MR. J. C. MURPHY
MR. W. R. BREWSTER	MR. STANLEY MCCANDLESS
MR. HENRY HUNT CLARK	MR. DONALD M. OENSLAGER
MISS ELEANOR DUNN	MR. W. A. PALLMÉ
MISS ELEANOR EUSTIS	MR. T. P. ROBINSON
MR. R. L. GUMP	MISS ELEANOR SAXE
MISS PAULINE HATFIELD	MR. A. H. STARKE
MR. W. BURTON WILSON	

INTRODUCTION
by Richard S. Kennedy

I

I first came across the manuscripts of *Welcome to Our City* in the Houghton Library over thirty years ago when I was doing research for a seminar in American literature. Since I was a young fellow just learning the scholarly trade and since I was an enthusiast about Thomas Wolfe, I became very excited: I thought I had discovered an unpublished work of primary importance. When I called it to the attention of Edward Aswell, the administrator of the estate of Thomas Wolfe, however, I found that Aswell was well aware of the play and had been trying to sell it to a Broadway producer for some time. In fact, Aswell so jealously guarded the text of *Welcome to Our City* against the day of a New York production that he would not let me quote a single line from it when I published my seminar paper as an article entitled "Thomas Wolfe at Harvard."

During my research into Wolfe's years of study and playwriting at Harvard, it became quite clear that *Welcome to Our City* was the best, by far, of the three full-length plays he had written during that period of apprenticeship, and I tried to find out as much as I could about how the play came into being, how successful it was when it was produced at Harvard in 1923, and why Wolfe had never found a commercial producer for it, either on Broadway or among the little theater groups. I interviewed eleven people who had taken part in the production, as well as a dozen others who had known Wolfe at the time or who had attended a performance of the play; and I combed through the letters and papers in the

Thomas Wolfe Collection of William B. Wisdom, which had recently been acquired by the Houghton Library. Little by little, an interesting story emerged.

Thomas Wolfe had come to Harvard Graduate School from the South in 1920 in order to work under George Pierce Baker in the 47 Workshop, which at that time was the most renowned playwriting program in the country. At first, Wolfe wrote plays about Appalachian mountaineers and later another about the Civil War period. But his genius finally awoke when he turned to the modern South as he knew it in his home town, Asheville, North Carolina, and dared to write about racial conflict, a subject mostly avoided by southern writers at that time. What really set him off, however, was something else: a sense of outrage over the real estate speculation and the civic boosterism that he had recently observed in Asheville.

Two years in Boston had begun to make him look at his native city with different eyes. Writing back home to a former teacher in 1922, he revealed how he felt after a summer spent in North Carolina and how he intended to express that feeling in his creative work:

> Coming home this last time I have gathered enough additional material to write a new play. . . . This thing I had thought naïve and simple is as old and as evil as hell; there is a spirit of world-old evil that broods about us, with all the subtle sophistication of Satan. Greed, greed, greed—deliberate, crafty, motivated—masking under the guise of civic associations for municipal betterment. The disgusting spectacle of thousands of industrious and accomplished liars, engaged in the mutual and systematic pursuit of their profession, salting their editorials and sermons and advertisements with the religious and philosophical platitudes of Dr. Frank Crane, Edgar A. Guest, and the American Magazine.

The play Wolfe began to write when he had just turned twenty-two centered on a scheme hatched by a group of real estate promoters who, together with other powerful figures in the community, contrive to buy up all the property in the centrally located Negro district. They plan to evict all the tenants, tear down the old houses, and build a new white residential section. When, under the leadership of a strong-willed doctor, the black population resists eviction, a race riot breaks out and leads to fire and bloodshed before it is put down by the state militia.

But Wolfe's social criticism did not confine itself to race relations and real estate speculation. The early 1920s was the era of Sinclair Lewis' *Main Street* and H. L. Mencken's attacks on the booboisie in *The Smart Set* magazine. Wolfe wanted to follow their example and include in his play satirical treatment of southern politicians, hypocritical religious leaders, anti-intellectual professors, civic boosters, provincial little theater groups, and the cultural barrenness of small-town life. As a result, the play presented a varied, though jumbled, picture of contemporary southern life.

Many details of the play were based solidly on reality. Wolfe took the Asheville scene and turned it into Altamont, peopling it with characters who, in some instances, bore a striking resemblance to certain Asheville citizens. But his central plot was entirely imaginary. There never had been a real estate conspiracy or a violent race riot in Asheville. About the closest situation in actuality to the real estate story was George Vanderbilt's purchase of 100,000 acres of farmland and forest when he established Biltmore House and its vast estate. For years, one old Negro man refused to sell his nine acres in the heart of the estate, although he was offered $10,000 for his property, worth at the time about $100. With this situation hovering in his memory, Wolfe developed his drama of the Altamont conflict provoked by a Negro doctor, owner of an antebellum mansion, who held out against the demands of the local white leaders.

When Professor Baker chose the play for production by the 47 Workshop in May of 1923, it was the most ambitious undertaking the group had ever attempted. With a cast of forty-five, the play included over thirty speaking parts and seven changes of set. But as a theatrical presentation it was far too long; thus began a struggle between Baker and Wolfe, first in conferences and later in rehearsals, to reduce its running time. Wolfe objected stubbornly to making the cuts and even threatened to withdraw the play, but finally he gave in because he did want to see his work staged. Still, he went about Harvard yard grousing to his friends that they were only going to see "a sliced version" of his play.

Although Baker insisted on a good deal of trimming, the play with its ten scenes, all but one requiring a change of set, lasted over three and a half hours in performance. The audience, people who came by invitation only and who were asked to write brief criticisms, complained about the length of the play, but most of the viewers found it an exciting theatrical evening. Indeed, the harshness of the satire and the forthright treatment of racial conflict even shocked some people who were accustomed to hearing drawing-room dialogue from the young Harvard playwrights. (Philip Barry's *You and I*, for example, had its first production in the 47 Workshop the previous year.) Yet in spite of its excessive length, some members of the 47 Workshop itself thought *Welcome to Our City* was the most important play that had ever appeared on their program.

After the performances, Baker was convinced that the play would be a success in New York if it were judiciously tightened, and he asked the Theatre Guild to give the play a reading. But Wolfe was unable to cut the play. That summer when he visited his fellow playwright, Henry Carlton, up in Madison, New Hampshire, Carlton outlined for him the number of plot threads he had introduced and pleaded with him to throw out two or three that were undeveloped or divergent. Listening to advice like this, Wolfe would solemnly agree, and after the Carlton family had retired, he would work late into the night: by morning he would have expanded one or more of his scenes with new dialogue. In his attempt to treat fully the varied life of a southern town, he thought he was creating a new form, and he refused, he told everyone, to make the play more "conventional." Instead of reducing the play in size, he restored most of the cuts that he and Baker had made in rehearsal, added further dialogue for some of his characters, inserted more topical satire, and sent the expanded version off to the Theatre Guild reader.

What had been in the Harvard production an unusual and provocative theatrical experience became in Wolfe's longer version a work in which dramatic development was frequently interrupted by digressive or static interchanges: Wolfe was striving to achieve either the wit of Bernard Shaw or the dreamy pathos of Eugene O'Neill, and not succeeding with either. Although he had polished up the dialogue in many places, he had ruined his play as a whole. Neither the Theatre Guild nor any of the other theater groups that gave his script a reading over the next few years was willing to take a chance on this unwieldy work or its stubborn author. As a consequence, Wolfe eventually turned away from the drama and began to write what he really had the talent to produce, prose narrative. Knowing as we do now that his energies brought forth such fictional works as *Look Homeward, Angel* and *The Web and the Rock*, we need not regret the outcome.

II

But what Wolfe could not do himself had been done for him, to some extent, by Professor Baker; and it has been my desire to rescue *Welcome to Our City* in the form that stimulated that audience of 1923. The version I have chosen for this publication is Wolfe's script of the play that Baker produced, and this creation of the 1920s can still make its impact on us now.

The story of the real estate scheme and the black resistance that erupts into urban riot is not out-of-date. Readers today will find in Wolfe's central plot an ominous echo of our own time when urban renewal projects drive poor black citizens out of prime areas that are then turned into high-rental properties for middle-class whites. On the other hand, the crude racial attitudes that the play reflects are very much outdated, and in order to respond to the play properly, we have to view this aspect of the work historically, recognizing that Wolfe was revealing not only his own racial prejudices and those of the South at that time but also the prevailing white attitudes all over the country. Even so, he still managed to create a drama that arouses an audience's sense of social justice and places its sympathies squarely on the side of the principal black characters.

The social satire too must be looked at in historical perspective; but once we give ourselves to the historical period in imagination, we find that the comic material carried along by this somber story is one of its principal appeals.

One additional feature of distinct literary interest that we should be aware of is the way in which Wolfe made use of expressionistic techniques. *Welcome to Our City* was written just as expressionism was beginning to make its impact on the American theater. Eugene O'Neill's *The Emperor Jones* and *The Hairy Ape* had their enormous success at the beginning of the 1920s, and Elmer Rice's *The Adding Machine* was just completing its New York run in the spring of 1923. Wolfe's play, with its musical motif of the "little futile piping tune" and the occasional stylized or exaggerated behavior of the characters, was looked upon by the 47 Workshop group as part of the modern movement, the breaking away from the standard realism of the American stage. This is why the theatrical historian Oliver Saylor, who saw a performance of *Welcome to Our City* in Cambridge, called it, in his book *Our American Theater*, "a play as radical in form and treatment as the contemporary stage has yet acquired." Actually, Wolfe's play is even more characteristic of the American handling of expressionism than O'Neill's work is. *Welcome to Our City* has the humor and high spirits that are distinctive features of such American expressionistic plays as John Howard Lawson's *Processional*, E. E. Cummings' *Him*, and Thornton Wilder's *The Skin of Our Teeth*—features which are lacking in their European predecessors.

Although the play reads very well in its shorter form, it is still rather long for stage presentation and would probably have to be cut for a theater audience—several of the talky exchanges curtailed and perhaps Scene 7 to be dropped in its entirety, a suggestion that Wolfe's advisors frequently made. But reading through the play, it is hard not to agree with Wolfe in his struggle to preserve the material. He was especially fond of Scene 7, "the cubistical, post-impressionist politician scene," as he called it, and the audience at Agassiz House Theater supported him in this feeling, for it is said that they found the conclusion of this scene (with the governor, undressed and toothless, reciting Shakespeare to himself in the mirror) the comic high point of the evening.

Perhaps if Edward Aswell had known of the existence of this shorter version of *Welcome to Our City*, he would have been able to place it with a theatrical producer. But with the long version of the play, he was not any more successful than Wolfe in convincing anyone of its possibilities. He eventually gave up, made a somewhat abridged version of it, and published that in *Esquire Magazine* in 1957. Nor could he interest any publisher in bringing out the play in book form.

Now that I have been given the opportunity to re-create the original production script, I feel that the discovery I made when I was a groping graduate student has at last been brought to light and made available for readers everywhere. I can even hope some day to see a well-cast, judiciously directed theatrical production, with, perhaps, a few revisions in dialogue imported from the later version. I think that Wolfe in his later years would have been pleased to see it too.

WELCOME TO OUR CITY

A Play in Ten Scenes

The Time is Summer, 1922

SCENE **1**

A street in Niggertown. One looks across at a ragged line of white-washed shacks and cheap one- and two-story buildings of brick. In the center is a vacant lot between the buildings. It is littered with rubbish, bottles, horseshoes, wagon wheels, and junk of every description.

A group of young negro men is pitching horseshoes in one part of the lot. In another, two young men are playing ball. Still else-where, another group is pitching pennies at a line drawn in the earth. To the right, there is a filthy looking restaurant. Through its dirty windows may be seen a long, greasy counter piled with quan-tities of fried food—chicken, fish, and meat. There are smeared glass cases, as well, which contain thick, pasty looking pies. A negro man and a stout negress are in attendance within.

Next door—divided only by a flimsy board partition—is a pool-room. It is a dark, fathomless place, in which men, seeming like ghosts, move through dense clouds of tobacco smoke around the green tables, under shaded lamps which cast wedges of sickly light upon them.

Farther up to the left, on the opposite side of the lot, is a moving picture theater, housed in a cheap building of whitewashed brick. The front of the theater is plastered with immense garish posters. One shows a woman jumping from a bridge onto a moving train; in another a horseman is taking a prodigious leap across the gap that yawns between two towering cliffs. A tinny automatic piano plays, ceases with a spasmodic jerk, hums ominously, and, without warn-ing, commences again.

At the extreme left is the side of a large brick building, which apparently fronts on a street in the white section. It is pierced by

windows, doors, and steps which lead down respectively into a bar-
ber shop, a pressing club, and a shoe-repair shop.

On the street are clustered groups of young negroes, some in
shirt-sleeves and suspenders, others more fashionably attired in box
coats with heavy stripes, flaring peg-top trousers and club-foot
shoes of a screaming yellow. Young negro women, attired in slouchy
finery, in which lavender predominates, and wearing coarse white
stockings and down-at-the-heel shoes, stroll by. The men make re-
marks which the girls answer freely. There is much ogling back and
forth, much laughter, a great deal of noise.

They are creatures of sudden whim, and do unexpected things.
Gales of merriment seize them; one will suddenly commence a shuf-
fling dance, and as suddenly end it. There is much rough horseplay
among the young men on the lot.

Up and down the street pass many people. Most of them are
young. Now and then, a more dignified or prosperous looking citi-
zen walks by. A stout, middle-aged negro, wearing a long frock coat
of good cloth and an expensive white vest, with a heavy gold chain,
passes. He addresses people right and left, bestowing genial greet-
ings or benedictions with a fat hand.

These circumstances, coupled with a pious smirk and the oiled
smugness of his bearing, cause us to suspect he is a minister of the
gospel. His thick lips are wreathed in smiles of sacrificial humility.
They move and murmur constantly. We do not hear what he is say-
ing to the people, but his mouth ever fashions and pronounces the
word "brother." And as he walks, from somewhere in the distance,
a foolish futile, ever-recurrent little tune is whistled, to which he
appears to keep step in his march onward across the stage. He
comes; he passes; and he goes; a leaping spark of rumour stills the
crowd, and treading on the heels of silence, the mortal kings and
captains of this earth march slowly past.

MR. HENRY (H. C.) SORRELL (White). [*Dictating at once to two*
    stenographers.] She's a bargain; she's a buy; and she's a

daisy! It can be done, if you have Vision—the motto of this office. Twenty-two hundred dollars a front inch until Thursday; price advances to three thousand then.

MR. J. C. DUNBAR (The Tailor). Done! I take it! How much down?

MR. HENRY SORRELL. $2.47—the rest in thirty days. [*Money is passed*]

MR. BURTON WEBB (Attorney and publisher). I'll give you twenty-five hundred, Jim. How much for a binder?

MR. J. C. DUNBAR. $1.63.

MR. BURTON WEBB. The trade's on. [*Money is passed*] She'll hit three thousand before the summer's over.

GOVERNOR PRESTON CARR. The State is a mighty empire, self-sufficient to all her needs. We are going Forward, not Backward; Service, Vision, Progress, Enterprise, the well-known Purity of our Womanhood. We can't lose! I'll give three thousand now.

MR. BURTON WEBB. Sold to Governor Preston Carr for three thousand dollars a front inch. Give me $2.30, please, Governor. [*Money is passed*]

MR. HENRY SORRELL. I offer $3500, Governor. What do you do?

GOVERNOR PRESTON CARR. Mr. Sorrell gets it. $3.11, please. [*Money is passed*]

MR. HENRY SORRELL. Buy and sell. Keep the ball rolling. Trade quick. That's the way to make it. [*They pass, and go.*]

MISS ESSIE CORPENING [*Twenty-three, mulatto, her saffron skin anointed, her slow cat's body wound in silken green; to Mr. J. C. Dunbar*]. Hello, Jimmy.

[*She enters with graceful loin movement the dark stair corridor above the drug store.*]

MR. J. C. DUNBAR [*laggard behind the host, drops farther back, turns, hangs, returns; with prankish schoolboy grin he en-*

ters too the corridor, hiding his face with his hat. Voice half up-stairs, neighing and palpitant]. Ess-see—who-o do-o you-u lo-o-ve?

[*The foolish, futile ever-recurrent little tune is whistled over again. The people, suspended in their acts, now break to movement. And suddenly, above the tumult of the crowd, one feels a great throbbing in the upper air, which is filled with the noise of whistles, the piercing blast of a siren, and the heavy, booming strokes of the courthouse bell. It is six o'clock.*

Soon the workmen begin to come by. They are big, strong men, with stooped, burly shoulders, and there is in their manner a solid weariness.

They march heavily and solidly on, each bearing a dinner pail or a lard bucket in his hand. They pay no attention to those on either side of them. Their hands and faces are covered with the dust of lime and cement, trenched and engraved by little streams of sweat, and their shoes and the bottoms of their trousers are stiff with mortar.

One of their number—a young negro—turns aside, going into the poolroom. Another pauses to talk to a negro in the vacant lot. The rest go solidly past, with an implacable, an animal power, paying no attention to those on either side of them.]

Curtain

SCENE **2**

*The office of the Altamont Development Company has been opened
by* MISS NEELY, *the stenographer, a girl of twenty-three years. She
is tall, blonde, slender and, to use a convenient label, "a true daughter of the South." She has "sweetness," but very little "light." We see
her as she is just completing a telephone conversation.*

MISS NEELY. Then you will be here at 10:15? . . . Yes . . . Mr.
Sorrell will be expecting you . . . Yes . . . Good-bye.
[*She hangs up the receiver.* DAN REED, *the office man, has just
entered. He is a fat, stupid looking negro, with a round, heavy,
but very good humored face.*]
DAN. Mawnin', Miss Helen.
MISS NEELY. Good morning, Dan. Mr. Sorrell left word that
you should come to his house as soon as you got here.
DAN [*Going*]. Yes'm.
MISS NEELY. And, oh, Dan. Will you get the mail from the
box when you come back? Here's the key. [*She gives it to
him.*]
DAN. Yes'm.
[*He goes out.* MISS NEELY *hastily looks over a memorandum as
her employer's clerk, picks up a sheaf of opened letters, and
comes down to her table, where she prepares to set to work.*

*There enters now an emaciated looking man of advanced mid-
dle age. He is of medium height and has thin, sharp features,
and sparse, greying hair. His skin is white, but there are red
spots on his cheeks. He is troubled by a little, dry cough, which
bothers him frequently and, after a spell of coughing, he wipes
his mouth and the end of his tongue carefully, and gazes intently into his handkerchief.*]

THE MAN. Good morning.

MISS NEELY. Oh, good morning, Mr. Jordan? That's the name, isn't it?

JORDAN. Yes. That's right. Is Mr. Sorrell in?

MISS NEELY. No, but I expect him any minute now. I know he wants to see you. Won't you wait?

JORDAN. Thank you. If it won't be long, I'll wait.

[*He sits down and has an attack of coughing which keeps him busy with his handkerchief.*]

MISS NEELY [*Casually, preoccupied with the memorandum*]. And how is your asthma this morning?

JORDAN. Bronchitis!

MISS NEELY. Of course! I knew it was one or the other. [*She calmly proceeds with her work, putting a sheet of paper on her machine.*]

JORDAN. I had a very bad night of it.

MISS NEELY. Really? I'm very sorry to hear it.

JORDAN. It was that miserable rain. Think of it! Three solid days of rain! Do you have weather like that often?

MISS NEELY [*Hastily*]. Oh, goodness, no! It's very seldom we have anything like it. It's high and dry here, you know. [*Rather proudly*]. We are 2300 feet above the sea level.

JORDAN. Yes, I know. Several people have told me. [*A pause, while she bends over to puzzle out some shorthand notes.*] You know, your people seem to have an extraordinary amount of information about the town.

MISS NEELY. Oh, everyone here is a booster for Greater Altamont. You'll get the fever too, if you stay long.

JORDAN. And what does Greater Altamont mean?

MISS NEELY. 100,000 by 1930. That's the goal we've set ourselves.

JORDAN. And after that, what? 200,000 by 1940, I suppose.

MISS NEELY. Why, yes. That's just it. You see, you are catching on already.

JORDAN [*Dryly*]. Yes. I think I get the idea.

MISS NEELY. Oh, it's easy to learn. And you've no idea how perfectly thrilling it is! It's like a big game in which everybody takes part. Everyone's working and boosting to make the town bigger and better.

JORDAN. The bigger, the better?

MISS NEELY. Why, of course. That's one of our slogans: Altamont—Bigger, Better, Brighter!

JORDAN. The town apparently is growing rapidly.

MISS NEELY. You've no idea how rapidly it has grown since the people woke up. It used to be such a sleepy, unprogressive sort of place. But everything's on the move now, I can tell you. Mr. Sorrell says we have a great future.

JORDAN. I am sure you will have only the biggest and best of everything—even of futures.

MISS NEELY. "It can be done!" That's the motto of this office. Mr. Sorrell says if you believe a thing hard enough, it will come true.

JORDAN. Why, come! The man's a philosopher.

MISS NEELY. He gave a talk at a Rotary Club Luncheon, and afterwards they adopted it as a slogan. "If you believe it, it's so." Mr. Sorrell really is a very progressive man.

JORDAN. With this inspired leadership I don't see how you can fail to reach your goal.

MISS NEELY. But you are going to be one of us, aren't you?

JORDAN [*With a smile*]. What must I do to become one "of you?"

MISS NEELY. Oh, that's easy. Just buy that pretty little house Mr. Sorrell showed you yesterday in Rutledge Park.

JORDAN. I would like to join your Club but your initiation fees are a bit steep, you know.

MISS NEELY [*As if repeating a memorized formula*]. Oh, but you can't lose on an investment in Altamont real estate. It keeps going up. And Rutledge Park is the most desirable section in the City. Mr. Sorrell said you could make a good turnover in six months if you wanted to.

JORDAN. Unfortunately, I am not interested in making a good turnover. What I am after is a home to live in. [*With a certain waspish good humor.*] I realize this puts me under suspicion here, but I assure you my species is not entirely extinct yet.

MISS NEELY. Oh, no. There are lots of people, nice people, too, right here in Altamont, who buy homes to live in.

JORDAN. You arouse my interest. I had not expected to find any so close at hand. I must look them up.

MISS NEELY. Of course, nearly everyone you meet *does seem* to be investing in something or other. Law used to be the great profession for the young men. Now they become real estate men, that is . . . . realtors.

JORDAN. I see. Every man his own agent.

MISS NEELY. What is your business, Mr. Jordan? Or have you retired?

JORDAN. I am a broken down writer looking for a roost. There you have me.

MISS NEELY. How perfectly thrilling! Do you write for the magazines?

JORDAN. Forty or fifty years ago, I did.

MISS NEELY. Did you ever try your hand at scenarios?

JORDAN. No! Oh, no! [*He mutters something under his breath that sounds like "God forbid."*]

MISS NEELY. I hear there's an awful lot of money in it. I'm writing one now. I'd like to show it to you when I get through and get your opinion.

JORDAN. Thank you. [*Feebly.*] I'll be glad to see it, of course.

MISS NEELY. Mercy! It must be perfectly gorgeous to be a writer. I know you're awfully good at it.

JORDAN. I thought so, too, once, twenty years ago. Now, I'm an antique—like Shakespeare.

MISS NEELY. Twenty years! Think of that. You must have made a fortune. I hear they pay five cents a word sometimes.

JORDAN. Few men in my profession buy homes in Rutledge Park,—even after twenty years. You know the prices out there are really outrageous.

MISS NEELY. But it's a very exclusive place, you see. Mr. Sorrell says that the price brings the right kind of people. It keeps out the Jews, he says.

JORDAN. I gather that it would—but please don't let me keep you from your work any longer.

MISS NEELY. I really don't know what can be keeping Mr. Sorrell. I can call his home, if you like?

[*She reaches toward the telephone.*]

JORDAN. Please don't trouble. He's doubtless on his way here now. Besides, I'm in no great hurry.

MISS NEELY. Then, just make yourself at home. This week's "Life" is on the table.

[*She proceeds with her typing.* JORDAN *looks over the litter of magazines on the table, tosses them aside, and, in a moment, strolls over to the windows where he stands looking out.*]

JORDAN [*Under his breath, but audibly*]. What a pity!

[*There enters now a short florid little man, who fairly bounces along with his energy and good spirits. He belongs to the great order of professional "boosters," people speak of him as a "hustler," a "live wire," as possessing the desirable qualities of "snap" and "ginger." The man is* JOSEPH BAILEY, *the Secretary of the Altamont Board of Trade. Show him a sunset, and he will translate it into terms of climate; a range of mountains and his mind leaps directly to statistics concerning hotels and tourists. So long have a "ready smile" and a "hearty handclasp" for everyone been part of his stock in trade that he really imagines he was born with a genius for good fellowship and kindliness. Active, vigorous, bustling, shallow, wholly engrossed in his little world of a tourist paradise, his constitutional insincerity is the most sincere and honest thing about him; once you learn to accept him on his own inflexible level you can observe him with all the awful fascination occasioned by a piece of mechanism which seems at times, supernaturally to transcend itself. He bears carefully under one arm an enormous silver cup, only the bottom of which is visible; the top is wrapped securely in brown paper. Though the morning is young, he wipes his forehead with a handkerchief as he enters! He is one of those persons who perspire freely.*]

BAILEY [*Cheerfully*]. Oh, good morning, Helen.

MISS NEELY. Oh, good morning, Mr. Bailey!

BAILEY [*Delivering himself rapidly*]. You are always the first on hand, I see! Good! Good! The sluggards who stay in bed miss half of life, I tell *you*! The glory of the Dawn is lost upon them. Oh, it is a joy to be abroad on a morning like this, filling your lungs with God's clean air, purified by an altitude of 2,300 feet. As I walked along this morning listening to the chirping of the little birds in the trees, I said to myself: "How good it is to be alive! How glad, how fortunate I am, to be living here in nature's wonderland, drinking its crystal water, breathing its bracing air, enjoying its healthful and—[*With a glance toward the stranger*]—health-restoring air. How little do we realize the treasures which are ours,—Helen, where can I put this cup?

MISS NEELY. Oh, it's Mr. Sorrell's cup, isn't it? Please take the wrapper off and let me see it. [*She attempts to take it off.*]

BAILEY. Ah, ah, ah, mustn't touch. Better get Mr. Sorrell to show it to you.

MISS NEELY. Put it here, then, on the table. This is Mr. Jordan, a prospective buyer. Mr. Jordan, this is Mr. Bailey, the Secretary of our Board of Trade.

JORDAN. I am glad to know you.

BAILEY. Welcome to our city! You will find the heart of Altamont as deep as a well, as wide as a barn door. That is the slogan which the Kiwanis Club has adopted. I am glad to know you, sir.

[*They shake hands.*]

JORDAN. Thank you. Everyone seems very friendly.

BAILEY. As I came in, I chanced to hear you say "What a pity!" Tell us what is a pity and we will change it for you.

JORDAN. I'm afraid you can't. That is your negro settlement, isn't it?

[*He points out the window.*]

BAILEY. Oh, *that*. My dear sir, I quite agree with you. It is an eyesore. "A Blot on the Scutcheon," as the Civitans call it.

JORDAN. I was thinking it was a pity that it should be here in the very heart of things, so to speak. You all seem to take such a pride in your city.

BAILEY. And justly so, I think. There is no cleaner or more beautiful town of its size anywhere.

JORDAN. The thing I don't understand is how you could have allowed it to happen. I think you have let the negroes have the best building site in your city.

BAILEY. You have hit the nail on the head! That is exactly what has happened! We awoke to our error too late.

JORDAN. I should say the town is pretty well built up. Any other development will have to take place at a considerable distance from the center of things.

BAILEY. Our progressive business men have decided that it is never too late to mend. I think I am violating no confidence when I tell you that steps are even now under way to do away with the negro settlement.

JORDAN. Do away with it?

BAILEY. That is, move it to a less conspicuous spot.—Out of sight, out of mind, you know. In that way all this section will become available for a first-class residential district, — finer even than Rutledge Park.

JORDAN. That strikes me as a rather tremendous undertaking.

BAILEY. The best interests of the community demand it. We no longer allow anything to stand in the way of progress in Altamont. As Mr. Rutledge himself said, the remedy in a case of this sort is surgery.

JORDAN. Your Mr. Rutledge seems to have an iron in almost every fire. Is he concerned in this new development?

BAILEY. Yes, indeed! He's the heaviest shareholder. [*To the typist*]. By the way, Helen, have they talked business with that nigger yet?

MISS NEELY. I got him on the 'phone this morning. He's coming in at ten o'clock.

BAILEY. That's splendid! Now things ought to move along. [*To Jordan*].We have a nigger doctor here who's one of the smoothest propositions you ever laid your eyes on. He's quite a fellow in many ways. He has his own car, you know, and holds his head up above the other darkies.

MISS NEELY. I think it's perfectly disgusting! You should see the airs his wife and daughter put on. They have a chauffeur, and go flying around just like white folks.

BAILEY [*Chuckling*]. Do they? Well! You know I've always said the nigger is the original missing link. He's like a monkey in many respects. He apes all the tricks of the white man. But Johnson's a good darkey and knows his place. Everyone here has a good word for him. I understand he's doing good work down there, too. You know, they live together like pigs.

JORDAN. Yes, I've heard conditions were pretty bad.

MISS NEELY. Oh, they're savages!

BAILEY. This darkey, by the way, is living in the old Rutledge home, the big house there at the top of the hill.
[*He points out the window*].

JORDAN. Yes, I have noticed it. A fine old house. It seems out of place in these surroundings.

BAILEY. The surroundings grew up around it. Mr. Rutledge inherited the place from his father's estate but the war ate up everything the family had. So Mr. Rutledge had to give the place up when he was a young man. Ever since he's wanted it back. It went against the grain, you see.

JORDAN. Yes, I can understand that it would. [*There is a pause.*] Then, there's something almost personal about the business, isn't there?

BAILEY [*Hesitating*]. Well, yes. But you can hardly blame the old boy for wanting the place back. His father was a slaveholder and a big man here in his day. The house has quite a history.

JORDAN [*Thoughtfully, gazing out the window*]. I wonder what he's going to do with it now: Do you think he'll go back there to live?

BAILEY. Oh, no! He has a big, fine house of his own,—a regular show place.

MISS NEELY. I shouldn't think he'd want to, now, anyway.

BAILEY. This is the last deal that stands in the way of the Development now. The company owns the whole works; what they didn't own they bought.

JORDAN. Then they are ready to go right ahead?

BAILEY. Oh, yes. They'll lose no time now. The whole scheme is coming out in tomorrow's papers. In fact, Mr. Rutledge hinted at it last night at the banquet. [*Importantly.*] Of course, only a few of us who were on the inside, so to speak, knew what he was driving at.

JORDAN. Yes. I read some account of the affair in the paper; a banquet in his honor, I believe?

BAILEY. Yes, sir. The Associated Civic Clubs, you know. They were all there:—the Rotary, The Kiwanis, the Civitans, the Baptist Ladies Social Union, the Y.M.C.A., the Junior and Senior Baracca, and Philathea, the Federated Woman's Clubs, the Fortnightly Discussion Society, the Friday Quill Club, and the Drama League. There were over five hundred people present. I never saw such enthusiasm! The scene beggared description!

JORDAN. Yes, so the paper said. Now that I think of it you took a leading part in the program yourself, didn't you?

BAILEY [*Modestly*]. Oh, not exactly. Just a filler-in, you know.

MISS NEELY. That's only his modesty. He was toastmaster.

BAILEY [*Coyly*]. Oh, I wish you hadn't mentioned that. It was nothing. [*With a modest laugh.*] Why, ha, ha,—I don't know yet why they singled me out.

MISS NEELY. And he presented the cup, too. That was the biggest event of the whole evening.

JORDAN. Oh, really? This cup? [*He indicates the package*].

BAILEY. Yes, sir. This is our Citizenship Cup. We originally intended to award it yearly to the citizen who has been of the greatest service to the community for the past year.

JORDAN. And Mr. Sorrell got it this year?

BAILEY. No, sir. Not this year, but for all time. He has permanent possession of it now. We saw nothing else to do; when a man has done as much for the town as he has there should be no strings tied to his honors. As I said in my little speech.

JORDAN. That was very well said.

BAILEY. He has been the moving spirit,—I used that phrase last night.

JORDAN. It's a good one. Spirit, surely, should not be without locomotion.

BAILEY. Yes, I think so, too. [*Oratorically and with appropriate gestures*] He has been the moving spirit in every constructive program of progress and growth which has changed this fair city of ours from a one-horse hamlet to the glittering gem of the Appalachians, the Mecca of the tourist, North and South. [*Lowering his voice*]. How was that?

JORDAN. Splendid, it should have brought the house down.

MISS NEELY [*Earnestly*]. Oh, it did, Mr. Jordan. I thought they'd never get done clapping.

BAILEY. You've really no idea how much that one man has done for this place. Rutledge Park alone has brought hundreds of people here to settle, first-class people, too, nothing shoddy about them. They all have their own cars.

MISS NEELY. I can remember when the Park was nothing but old bare fields and meadows; it hasn't been long.

BAILEY. Why it hasn't been ten years. That's nothing! I can remember when the ground this building stands on was used as a cow pasture. And then one man comes along and shows us what we can do with a little enterprise— and look at us! We're growing faster today than any town in the State.

JORDAN. I think I understand your enthusiasm. Your friend Sorrell has not only made money, he has shown other people how to make it.

BAILEY. That's it exactly. He had Vision.

JORDAN. I beg your pardon?

BAILEY. I say he had vision, the thing big business men, and poets, and all those people have, you know.

JORDAN. Oh.

BAILEY. Yes—and faith, that's what it was,—faith.

JORDAN. The thing preachers and all those people have?

BAILEY. Yes,—And imagination! He had that, too.

JORDAN. Really, I don't see why someone hasn't written him up for the American Magazine. There's material here for another outpouring of the industrial muse; the Romance of Big Business, and that sort of thing, you know?

BAILEY [*Excitedly*]. Helen, why haven't we thought of that? It's a wonderful idea; think of the publicity. Who could we get to do it for us?

MISS NEELY. Why not ask Mr. Jordan? He's a writer.

BAILEY. You? Why this is wonderful—an act of Providence. You're the very man!

JORDAN [*Feebly*]. No, no, you'd better ask someone else. I don't do this sort of thing.

[*At this moment* SORRELL *comes in. He is a rather countrified looking man in the thirties, sleek, shiny, self-satisfied and bearing himself with smug good humour and affability.* BAILEY *rushes toward him quivering and incoherent with excitement.*]

BAILEY. Sorrell, Sorrell.—The American Magazine, faith, vision, imagination, publicity, think of it!

SORRELL [*Impatiently*]. Oh, tell me some other time, Joe, I'm very busy this morning. I'm already late for an engagement with this gentleman. Good morning, sir. [*Shakes hands with* JORDAN.] I'm very sorry to have kept you waiting.

JORDAN. The time has passed very pleasantly with Mr. Bailey.

SORRELL. Joe's a good fellow but he gets in the way sometimes.

BAILEY. He calls me Joe and I call him Henry. That's the way it is between us. We're both members of the Rotary Club, you know, and everyone calls each other by his first name.

JORDAN. That's very friendly of you.

BAILEY. Isn't it?

SORRELL. Helen, have there been any calls?

MISS NEELY. No, sir. I got that man Johnson on the 'phone. He said he'd be here at ten-fifteen.

SORRELL. Good. [*He looks at his watch.*] That gives me over an hour. [*To Jordan.*] If you'll excuse me for a few minutes while I make a telephone call—

JORDAN. Certainly. I've been hearing the history of Altamont, I find it very interesting.

SORRELL. Oh, you'll find Joe full of facts and figures. He'll tell you anything you want to know. He's our little walking encyclopedia.

[*To Miss Neely.*] I'm calling Mr. Rutledge. I'll use the other phone.

[*He goes into the inner office and closes the door behind him.*]

BAILEY. Now—where are you staying, Mr. Jordan?

JORDAN. For the present, at the Inn.

BAILEY. The Inn, I must get that down. [*He takes out a notebook and makes a jotting.*] Beautiful place, the Inn. It cost over three quarters of a million dollars and that was ten years ago, when materials were low. I want to come around sometime and have a good long chat with you.

JORDAN. I shall be delighted, of course.

BAILEY. I want to take you out and show you all the points of interest. I have a car, you know.

JORDAN. Oh, really?

BAILEY [*Comfortably*]. Yes, I have a car, I couldn't get along without it now.—Now, about the article for the American Magazine, how soon could you have that ready for us?

JORDAN. I think you'd better find someone else, who has all the facts.

BAILEY. Oh, I can furnish all the facts.

JORDAN. Yes, but, you see, this sort of thing is not in my line. [*He hesitates.*] Besides, I'm here to rest. My health is not good.

BAILEY [*Staring at him intently*]. Oh!

JORDAN [*Hastily*]. Chronic bronchitis, you know.

BAILEY. Oh!

JORDAN. Nothing pulmonary, you understand? The doctor assures me of that.

BAILEY [*Still staring*]. Yes, of course. Oh, yes. Certainly not. [*Briskly.*] Well, sir, you have come to the right place. We have lots of people who come here with chronic bronchitis. There's nothing like our climate for it.

JORDAN. Yes, high and dry, the doctor says. What is the exact altitude?

[*This proves fatal.* BAILEY *inflates his chest, throws one foot briskly forward, and delivers himself as follows:*]

BAILEY. Altamont, a city of some 30,000 souls, is situated on the crest of a plateau 2,300 feet above the level of the ocean. Toward the setting sun stretches away the illimitable vistas of the western peaks, and the towering summits of the Pisgah range, lapt continually in fleecy clouds; to the south the blue glory of the Black Mountain presents itself to the dazzled eyes of the spectator, to the West the sheer wall of the Blue Ridge charms and enthralls. Wooded peaks of unparalleled majesty and beauty. Crystal streams, as yet unpolluted by human touch, broken only by the sportive antics of the mountain trout, virgin forests, where the foot of man has never trod, all conspire to give to this favored region the title of "Nature's Wonderland." The climate—

JORDAN [*Desperately*]. Yes, yes, I know about the climate. It is very healthful, I am told.

BAILEY [*Proceeding with firmness and determination*]. The climate is high, dry and salubrious. The rigors of a northern winter are tempered with the exotic warmths of the tropics; there are few days so cold that the wearing of overcoats is necessary, few nights so warm but that blankets may be used with perfect comfort. A little to the south is the great isothermic belt, famous for its ruddy grapes, and its equable temperatures. The mean average temperature is 61 degrees, the mean average rainfall is— [*He hesitates.*] I've forgotten for the moment, but I can find it in Sorrell's desk. [*He begins to frantically displace the papers on Sorrell's desk.*]

JORDAN [*Softly and entreatingly under his breath*]. My God! My
   God! My God!

MISS NEELY [*Springing up*]. Mr. Bailey, what are you doing?

BAILEY. The mean average rainfall; quick, where is it? You
   know—the little book.

MISS NEELY. Oh, let it go, please! I'll get the blame now for
   disturbing these papers! [*She begins to arrange them in their
   proper order again.*]

BAILEY. It has escaped my mind for the present, but it will
   return—it will return.

JORDAN [*Weakly*]. Never mind. You can tell me later.

MISS NEELY. Yes, talk to him about something else. Tell him
   about the town instead of the scenery. It makes less
   trouble.

BAILEY [*Pondering in vexation*]. Rainfall—rainfall,—I had it on
   the tip end of my tongue—never mind. It will come
   back.

JORDAN. You have a theatre, I suppose, among your other
   treasures.

BAILEY. A theatre! My dear sir, we have *four* theatres!

JORDAN [*Surprised*]. That is really remarkable in a town of
   this size.

BAILEY [*With enthusiasm*]. I tell you we have everything the
   larger cities have. You'll never want for a place to go
   here. You can see a new show every day, if you want
   to.—Helen, how often do they change the pictures?

MISS NEELY. Three times a week at the Bijou, Olympic, and
   Orpheum; every day at the Princess.

BAILEY [*Triumphantly*]. You can see two shows a day if you
   want to. Think of that! And I can remember this town
   when there was no place to go to, nothing to do! People
   stayed at home at night and read.

JORDAN. A bad state of affairs.

BAILEY. I can remember this town when it was no more than

a country village. Saturday was a big day because the
farmers drove in and livened things up a bit. Look at us
today!

JORDAN. Your growth is remarkable, surely.

BAILEY. Facts talk! Figures don't lie! We have eight schools,
one of which cost over a half a million dollars, six banks,
nine big hotels, over two hundred inns and boarding
houses, and twenty-three churches, one of which cost
half a million. Our land values are the highest in the
state, our per capita wealth the greatest; we have over
four thousand private-owned motor cars and over sixty-
three miles of paved streets within our city limits. What
does all this show?

JORDAN. I have no idea.

BAILEY. Progress, Progress, Progress!!!

[SORRELL *returns from the inner room.*]

SORRELL [*Rather impatiently*]. Oh, haven't you gone yet, Joe?
Go along now. I'll see you later.

BAILEY. I thought I'd go along with you and Mr. Jordan and
show him a few points of interest.

SORRELL [*With resignation*]. Oh, all right, if you don't talk us
to death.

[*To Jordan.*] I've just been talking to Mrs. Porter—the
woman who owns the house we looked at yesterday.

JORDAN. Yes?

SORRELL. She has decided not to sell, I am sorry. You never
know when these women will change their minds.

[JORDAN *coughs into his handkerchief.*]

SORRELL. Now, I have something in mind for you that I think
will be just the thing you want.

JORDAN [*Staring into his handkerchief*]. Perhaps, a rented house
will be the thing I want.

SORRELL. But I thought you said—[*He looks at him hard.*] We
will talk of that too. [*Smoothly*] This place I am showing

you is in a good neighborhood, a little old-fashioned perhaps, but with nice friendly people as neighbors. Very
convenient and close in.

BAILEY. Oh, you will find that people here can't do enough
for you. If you take sick, there will be someone at your
bedside day and night.

JORDAN. I'm sure that is very considerate of them. [*To Sorrell*]
Shall we go now? I'm a little tired.

SORRELL. Yes, certainly, I'll be right along. Joe, take Mr. Jordan down and put him in my car.

JORDAN. Then—good-bye, Miss Neely.

MISS NEELY. Good-bye. But you'll come in again, won't you?

JORDAN. It will always be a pleasure, Miss Neely.
[*He shakes hands with her and goes out with* BAILEY. SORRELL
stays behind a moment.]

SORRELL [*Confidentially. Lowering his voice*]. Helen, I have
been talking with Mrs. Porter. It's too bad! She won't sell
Jordan the house. The people in that neighborhood simply won't stand for it!

MISS NEELY. But why? He seems a very nice man.

SORRELL [*Glancing swiftly down the hall and then speaking sharply
behind his hand*]. Lunger!

MISS NEELY [*With a gasp of horror*]. Oh!

BAILEY'S VOICE [*Down the hall*]. Hurry up, Henry.

SORRELL [*In a cheerful voice*]. All right, gentlemen, I'm coming. [*He goes out down the hall.*]

BAILEY'S VOICE. I was telling him he won't know himself in a
month. This air works wonders—[*The clang of the elevator
door shuts off his conversation.*]

MISS NEELY [*As before*]. Lunger!
[*She wipes hard, with her handkerchief the hand which the
stranger had just grasped.*]

Curtain

SCENE **3**

The office again. It is now ten o'clock.

An old man, gaunt, stooped, palsey-shaken, and leaning on a gnarled cane, enters the office. He is on the seamy side of seventy, yet one perceives in him a certain tenacious vitality which may enable him to hang on to life for a good many years longer; he is a creaking gate which hangs by one hinge, but which hangs, *nevertheless. His voice is high, quavering, irascible; a certain impediment in the speech thickens and renders indistinct his conversation. He has long bedraggled white mustaches, heavily streaked with tobacco juice.*

SORRELL *enters the office from the corridor.*

SORRELL [*Rather irritably*]. Good morning, father.

OLD SORRELL. Good mornin', Henry.

SORRELL [*Seating himself at his desk*]. Well? . . . . . What can I do for you?

OLD SORRELL. I jest thought I'd come in out o' the sun fer a spell. It's hotter'n blazes out in the square.

SORRELL [*Showing his irritation*]. I'm very busy this morning, father.

OLD SORRELL [*Flying into a rage at once*]. Oh, I kin go! I kin go! I got too much pride to stay where I'm not wanted. I was good enough to go all through the Civil War and git a bullet hole in the roof o' my mouth big enough to stick yore fist through—[*Here he opens his toothless mouth and sticks his finger into the gap.*]—but I ain't good enough now to be treated decent when I come to my own son's office. [*Shaking his finger.*] Let me tell you somethin'—

SORRELL [*Wearily*]. Yes, I know. I know, father—but the Civil War was over fifty years ago. We're living in different times today.

OLD SORRELL. You—what have you ever done, sir? Sit aroun' in an office all your life an' you think you can talk back to a man who went all thru the Civil War. Have you got any bullet holes in you? Have you?

SORRELL [*Trying to pacify him*]. No, but—

OLD SORRELL. Then don't argue with me! You ain't been nowhere an' you ain't seen nothing! Lookee thar! [*Again he stretches his mouth open to the cracking point, and sticks his finger in.*] Hole's big enough to stick your fist through. All the doctors who ever seen it say it's a miracle I lived to tell the story!

[AMOS TODD, *an old negro man with a very kindly face, enters the office.*]

AMOS. Mo'nin', boss.

SORRELL. All right, Amos. Just sit down. I'll see you in a minute.

OLD SORRELL. No! You've got no place fer yore ole father, but the fust dirty nigger that comes in you ask to have a seat as nice as you please.

AMOS [*Backing away nervously*]. Dat's all right, boss. I jest came caze I got dealin's wid him.

OLD SORRELL [*Advancing toward him, brandishing his cane*]. Don't you give me none o' your sass, you dirty nigger.

SORRELL [*Stepping between*]. You leave him alone, Father. He's said nothing to you.

OLD SORRELL [*Storming and fuming about the place*]. By God! I ain't goin' to take nothin' off a damn nigger. I fought all thru the Civil War, an' I got this to show for it. [*He again opens his mouth and inserts his finger, speaking in almost inarticulate fashion.*] Lookee there! Big enough to stick your hull fist through.

AMOS [*Sliding towards the door*]. I'll come in agin, boss.

SORRELL. Stay where you are, Amos. [*He takes a bill from his pocket and slips it into his father's hand.*] Come back when I'm not so rushed, Father.

OLD SORRELL [*Pocketing the money and grumbling*]. All I got to say is, this ain't no way to treat a Civil War vet'ran what's got a hole in his mouth big enough to stick yore—[SORRELL *pushes him gently out of the office, still talking angrily—as he disappears he again turns, sticks his finger in his mouth, and mumbles.*] "Lookee there."

AMOS [*Chuckling*]. De ole ginlemen gits powful upsot, don' he?

SORRELL. He's in his dotage, Amos.

AMOS. Sho! Yo don' tell me.

[SORRELL *goes to his desk and busies himself with some letters there. Presently* MR. RUTLEDGE, *a fine courtly man, just above sixty years, comes in. Occasionally in speech and manners he betrays by some rhetorical gesture, long years of practice as a courtroom lawyer. Ordinarily a man of composure and suavity, he shows a certain restrained nervousness which leads one to deduce the impending presence of an important event. He greets Amos with a casual affection which the old man returns in a way that sufficiently indicates his respect and veneration.*]

RUTLEDGE. Good morning, Amos. You're looking well.

AMOS. Jes' tolable, Marse. Dis heah mis'ry in mah back's been plaguin' me agin. I reckon I ain't got much mo' time on dis airth.

RUTLEDGE. Go on, Amos. They'll have to shoot you on Judgment Day.

[*The old man chuckles in a slow, heaving fashion, and is very much pleased.*]

SORRELL. Good morning, sir. I tried to get you on the phone but they told me you were at court.

RUTLEDGE. Yes. I had a case of theft. A young nigger broke into a pressing shop and stole a suit of clothes. Six years at State Prison.

SORRELL. That's pretty tough!

RUTLEDGE. No, pretty good, I think. Burglary's a capital crime in this state. He came off light. He'll be only twenty-four when he comes out, and it will take him away from that crowd he's running with. Amos, what's wrong with these young bucks nowadays?

AMOS [Shaking his head]. Oh. Lawd, marse, dey's a mean good-for-nothin' bunch. Dey needs someone to git after dem with a stick. Dat's what. [He wags his head and mutters ominously to himself.]

SORRELL. Well, that's the end of Court for this session, isn't it?

RUTLEDGE. Yes, that finishes it.

SORRELL. I'm glad of it. There are a number of matters I want to talk over with you.

RUTLEDGE. I'm dog-tired, but go ahead.

AMOS. Marse!

RUTLEDGE. What are you waiting for, Amos? [Remembering] Oh, give it to him, Sorrell. Don't plague the old man so. [Sorrell produces a check from his pocket and gives it to the negro.]

AMOS [Taking it gingerly between his fingers]. What's dis heah?

SORRELL. Go easy with that, Amos; it's worth two thousand dollars.

[The old man hastily thrusts it back at Sorrell with shaking fingers.]

AMOS. Heah! I don' want dis boss, I mowt lose hit.

SORRELL. No one can get the money on it but you, Amos. That's a certified cashier's check payable to you.

AMOS. Cain't I have de money instid?

RUTLEDGE. They'll give you the money at the bank. You don't want to go walking around with two thousand dollars in your pocket, do you?

AMOS. I'se skeard to trust myse'f wid hit. [*At this moment* DAN REED *returns with the mail which he hands to* SORRELL.]

SORRELL. I tell you what I'll do, Amos. I'll get Dan here to take you to the bank. He'll get it cashed for you. [*He gives the check to Dan Reed.*]

AMOS [*Grabbing for it*]. Heah, niggah, you gib dat to me.

SORRELL. Why, you trust Dan, don't you?

AMOS. I don't trust no niggah, boss, let alone dese young 'uns.

[DAN REED *makes shuffling movements with his feet as if about to depart with the treasure.*]

SORRELL. Look out Amos! There he goes!

AMOS [*Handling his cane and stamping forward*]. Come back heah, niggah, dis minnit! I'll cane you ovah de haid if you don't!

RUTLEDGE. Give it to him Dan, and don't bother him any more. [DAN *does so.*] Now take him down to the Bankers' Trust and make a deposit for him. Amos, what are you going to do with all this money?

AMOS. I don' know, marse. Seems to be pow'ful lot fo' an' ole niggah lak me, but vittles comes high.

SORRELL. Well, you're a good trader, Amos. We paid you the top price for that shack of yours.

AMOS. Mebbe so, boss, but I lived dere goin' on fo'ty years now. Dat place seem lak home to me.

RUTLEDGE. Amos, I think you know that I shall always be your friend.

AMOS. Why, marse, I 'member de day you was bawn. Mistah Johnny comes out ter de gahden—

SORRELL. Who's Mister Johnny?

RUTLEDGE. That was my father.

SORRELL. Go on Amos! You're not that old.

AMOS. I'se gittin' powful ole, boss.

SORRELL. How old!

AMOS. I dunno. Way ovah a hund'ed, I spec.

[SORRELL *smiles, but* RUTLEDGE *silences with a gesture*].

RUTLEDGE. You're a good old man, Amos, no matter what your age is. I wish there were more of your kind left. [*Regretfully.*] Eh, Lord! Those days are gone. There aren't many darkies left like you, Amos.

AMOS. Dey took a stick to us, marse, an' made us behave. Dat's what dese young niggahs need. Dey go flyin' round gittin' demselves mixed up in scrapes like that gran' son o' mine.

RUTLEDGE. Where is that boy, Amos?

AMOS. He's on the gang . . . de good fo' nothin' thing. Dat's whar! He gits out nex' week, but dey'd bettah keep 'im whar he b'longs an' save demselves trouble.

RUTLEDGE. Now, Amos, let me give you a word of advice. I hope you'll take part of this money and fix up your shoe shop. Put in new equipment, and get a couple of young men to help you. It will pay you in the long run.

AMOS. Mebbe, marse, mebbe, I dunno. Livin' comes high.

SORRELL. Take him out, Dan.

DAN. Yes, sah. [*They go out. There is a silence a moment.* MR. RUTLEDGE *seems lost in reverie.*]

SORRELL. A good old man.

RUTLEDGE [*Starting*]. What? Yes—I was thinking, Sorrell, on the everlasting queerness of things. I was thinking that I might be taking money from the hand of Amos, instead of him from me.

SORRELL. But that's impossible.

RUTLEDGE. Ah, Sorrell, a great many things are possible. I never thought I'd see the day we bought property from one of my father's slaves. Think of that!

SORRELL. Yes, sir—Now about this matter of Johnson's house—

RUTLEDGE [*Stung by the word and speaking for the first time with considerable passion*]. My house, Sorrell! My house—mine! Do you hear? [*Displaying considerable agitation, he turns abruptly and walks to the window.*]

SORRELL. I'm sorry I used that word, Mr. Rutledge.

RUTLEDGE. It's all right, Sorrell. I am not myself these days.

SORRELL. This long session has upset you. [*With great smoothness*] What I meant to say was the house which is spiritually yours but which, by dint of circumstances over which we had no control, has temporarily passed into other hands.

RUTLEDGE [*Throwing back his head and laughing gaily*]. My dear boy, why aren't you holding office? [*He becomes serious again and a trifle grim in his manner as he looks out of the window.*] Try as I may, Sorrell, try as I may—By God it goes against the grain!

SORRELL [*Soothingly*]. I know, sir, I know. I quite appreciate your feelings.

RUTLEDGE. No, you don't Sorrell. No one can appreciate my feelings. No one can understand the bitterness and despair in the heart of that boy who stood by helpless, while the house of his people was debauched before his eyes!

SORRELL [*Alarmed*]. Mr. Rutledge, you really shouldn't let yourself go like this!

RUTLEDGE. But no one can say I have any bitterness towards these people. If they say that, they lie.

SORRELL. Oh, no, indeed, Mr. Rutledge, everyone knows what a generous friend you have been to them. The best people of both races know it. Your gifts to the Industrial School, to Calvary Church, to—

RUTLEDGE [*Waving his hand*]. All right, all right, I've talked too much. This day has meant too much to me.

SORRELL. I think we all understand the importance of the occasion. The whole success of the Development depends
upon this trade.

RUTLEDGE. Yes, Sorrell, the whole success of the Development—and more—for we are buying back a kingdom today, my friend. We are buying back a treasure of memo-
ries and romance, so delicate, so rare, so far removed
from this obscene push, that I almost hold my breath
whenever I think of it. It's not dead! It sleeps—the one
thing I yet dream of.

SORRELL [*Tactlessly*]. Will you go back there to live now?

RUTLEDGE [*With a deep, wounded cry*]. My God, man, why did
you say that? [*A profound pause*]. Oh, Sorrell, you must
bear with me. I'm not myself today.

[*Young* LEE RUTLEDGE *enters. He is a handsome, erect, some-*
what pampered fellow of twenty-five years, with finely cut fea-
tures and straw-colored hair.]

LEE. Good morning, Father.

RUTLEDGE. Good morning, son.

SORRELL. How are you, Lee?

LEE [*Coldly*]. Fine, thanks.

RUTLEDGE. Where is your mother?

LEE. She's down town shopping. I left her at the Bon Marche.
I'm to drive down and get her at noon. Are you coming
home for lunch?

[SORRELL *goes into the inner room.*]

RUTLEDGE. No. I'll lunch in town today. I'm very busy.

LEE. Then I'll be on my way.

RUTLEDGE [*Recalling him*]. Oh, son!

LEE. Yes, sir?

RUTLEDGE. How much time have you before you go back to
college?

LEE. Only two weeks now.

RUTLEDGE. Are you having a good time?

LEE. Great, Father.

RUTLEDGE. That's good. I want you to have a good time you know. [*Hesitates.*] Sit down a moment, Lee. I want to talk to you.

LEE. I'm in a big hurry. Mother will be waiting you know.

RUTLEDGE. Let her wait then. This is more important. [LEE *sits down.*] There's one thing I regret about your summer, Lee.

LEE [*Looking at him sharply*]. What is that?

RUTLEDGE. I haven't seen as much of you as I wanted.

LEE [*Rather uncomfortably*]. Well, Father, you know you've been awfully busy this summer, what with one thing and another.

RUTLEDGE. That's true, son. But I'd have spared you the time if you'd come to me.

LEE. You know how it is, Father. I hate to bother anyone I see is busy—and worried. And then lately, when I thought I would, you've been in court so much.

RUTLEDGE. But son, that's the very time I'd like to have seen you. You're coming right into my office when you finish your course and it wouldn't hurt to learn a little of court procedure now.

LEE [*Uncomfortably*]. I guess that's right.

RUTLEDGE. Lee, I don't want you to think I don't like your friends. You go with a nice set of young people, I know, and that's right. I want you to hold your head up; you've a right to. Your family is as good as any. But don't become too exclusive, son, or rather, don't let people think you are. You ought to mix around and meet more people. You'll need that later on.

LEE. You mean farmers and countrymen, and people like that?

RUTLEDGE. Why not? That's the stuff that makes up the population.

LEE. Well, I think I'll be doing enough if I know the law when I start in practice.

RUTLEDGE. My dear boy, let me tell you something I had to learn with bitter experience. It is important to know the law; but it is indispensable to know the jury. [*He gets up and puts his hand on the boy's shoulders affectionately.*] Now I don't want you to think that's hard or cynical. We'll keep this between ourselves, but we'll face the facts, won't we, and prepare to meet them?

LEE. Yes, sir.

[SORRELL *returns. During the conversation with Sorrell,* LEE *shows indifference, almost dislike, of the other's smug manner.*]

SORRELL. Oh, Lee, you must get in more often. We're always glad to see you.

LEE. Thanks. [*He starts to go out*].

SORRELL [*Confidentially, drawing him to one side*]. Lee, just a word with you. I couldn't help noticing you don't attend Church as regularly as you once did. [*With fat good humor.*] Now, I know how it is, my boy. I've been young too. It's very pleasant I know, and a great temptation to go out to the Country Club on Sunday morning to play tennis with a pretty girl [*Solemnly*] but I want to tell you this, Lee, you're coming back here soon to take up your father's profession and to mix in with the business men here. Lee, you'll have to attend church regularly if you want to prosper. You can't meet the right kind of people otherwise. Church membership is a business asset these days, and you can't afford to overlook it. I want to tell you, from my own experience, you can do little or nothing until you have accepted Jesus Christ as your Saviour.

LEE [*Rather curtly*]. Thank you, I guess you are right. Well, father, I'll tell mother you're not coming. Good-bye.

RUTLEDGE. Good-bye, son. [LEE *goes out.*] Now to the details of this business. Has a deed of sale been made out?

SORRELL. Helen is filling in the forms now. [*He nods toward the inner office.*]

RUTLEDGE [*In grim set tones*]. If he should balk?

SORRELL. He can't! He can't. Do you think he could stand up against the public opinion in this matter? I tell you, sir, the town is simply wild with enthusiasm. There's been nothing like it before.

RUTLEDGE. They say he's a smart man.

SORRELL. For a negro, yes.

RUTLEDGE. He's a mulatto. There's a difference.

SORRELL. Yes. [*Lowering his voice and speaking in a loud whisper, after looking around cautiously.*] You know, they say his mother—

RUTLEDGE. Oh, don't whisper, man! Where is your secret? His mother was as black as the ace of spades and everybody's woman. Is that a world's wonder?

SORRELL. She was murdered, wasn't she?

RUTLEDGE. Yes, in a drunken row, I believe. But the man deserves all the more credit, coming as far as he has. He must have had a hard row to hoe. I wonder how he did it!

SORRELL. Some fraternal organization sent him to their orphanage and schooled him, I am told. From there he went to some negro institute and then north to study medicine.

[*There enters, now, a tall, rather gaunt appearing man, at least fifty years old, but very erect and vigorous looking. He has the prominent high boned features of a Scotchman, rather obstinate, but yet finely molded lines in his face, a tight mouth and aquiline nose, which gives him a scholarly appearance. He has deep hollows in his cheeks, and bright, thirsty looking eyes.*]

Hello! It's Mr. McIntyre.

RUTLEDGE. Good morning, McIntyre. [*In a cordial manner.*]

MCINTYRE [*Coldly*]. Good morning, Henry, here are the keys to my house. I hope you have occasion to use them soon.

[RUTLEDGE *during this conversation half sits on the table swinging one leg under him, and turning the pages of a magazine.*]

SORRELL. Is everything in order?

MCINTYRE [*With a wintry smile*]. Everything. The kettles are on the stove. A tenant can move in at any time, if you find one.

SORRELL. Good. Now don't you worry a particle. Pretty little place like that don't go begging long. We'll get you a very favorable price, Professor.

MCINTYRE. I hope so, Henry. [*Pause*] The truth is, that house is almost all I have, and I'm pressed for funds, so the sooner the better.

SORRELL. When do you leave for your new school?

MCINTYRE. This afternoon at four-fifteen.

RUTLEDGE. [*Looking up*]. Then I hope you'll let Lee run you down to the station.

MCINTYRE. Thank you. That won't be at all necessary. My baggage is already there. So I won't put you to that trouble.

RUTLEDGE. Oh, it's no trouble at all. [*He goes back to his reading.*]

SORRELL. Well, Professor, I'm sorry to see you go.

MCINTYRE. Yes, Henry, I think you are.

SORRELL. Of course we old students understood that you aren't the radical they said you are. But people don't understand these things. They get around and talk. You've got to be careful about people, Professor.

MCINTYRE [*Quietly*]. Yes, Henry, you've got to be careful about people.

SORRELL. As far as I'm concerned, I'd like you to stay on here forever. You seemed to fit the job.

MCINTYRE. I've been here many a year, Henry. My roots grew very deep.

SORRELL. I've always said, Professor, that you were the right man in the right place. Of course I didn't take the Latin any longer than I had to, and I think you were wrong about the Greek—

MCINTYRE. A classical scholar is born, not made—Nascitur non fit, henricus.

SORRELL. Of course,—Well, I suppose I'm doing about as well as those that took all that stuff.

MCINTYRE. I'm sure you are.

SORRELL. I don't believe most of those fellows amount to much anyway. But I really think I got a great deal out of the Manual Training and the Shorthand, and you had a good influence on all the boys. I'll say that for you, Professor.

MCINTYRE. Thank you, Henry. That's very kind of you. And now I'll tell you good-bye. You have my address and know what to do in case of a trade.

SORRELL. Yes—Well then I suppose the best of friends must part, mustn't they? Good-bye sir, and good luck to you [*They shake hands and* MCINTYRE *turns to go*].

RUTLEDGE [*Getting up from his table*]. Just a moment, McIntyre. There is something I want to say to you.

MCINTYRE. Do you think, sir, there is anything we can say to each other?

RUTLEDGE. Yes, I do. I am sorry to see that you feel differently.

MCINTYRE. I feel there is no possible ground on which we can meet.

[*There is dead silence a moment. Finally*—]

RUTLEDGE. That's definite enough, certainly. I suppose I ought to let the matter drop on that, but I am interested in knowing the reason for all this. You will pardon my saying so, but it seems as I have every right to expect your friendship.

MCINTYRE. And what makes you think so?

RUTLEDGE. At the time when sentiment was hottest against you, I came to your aid, at the expense of considerable personal criticism. I opened a way by which you could escape your difficulties.

MCINTYRE. You opened a way that was a dishonor and an insult.

RUTLEDGE. Man! Do you not know that everything in a matter of this sort depends upon a compromise?

MCINTYRE. There can be no compromise upon the ground of truth.

RUTLEDGE. I know it is useless to convince you.

MCINTYRE. The Scotch are a stubborn people, Mr. Rutledge. [BAILEY *comes bouncing in.*]

BAILEY. Good morning, everybody. Henry, are you going to the Rotary luncheon today?

SORRELL. Yes, yes, yes! Only for heaven's sake, leave me alone till then. Can't you see we are busy?

BAILEY [*Cooly*]. All right. I'll meet you at noon and drive you down in my car. Good morning, Mr. Rutledge. Congratulations.

RUTLEDGE. Thank you, Bailey.

BAILEY. And when do you leave us, Professor?

MCINTYRE. Today.

BAILEY. Where did you say you are going?

MCINTYRE [*Coldly*]. I don't think I said.

BAILEY. Oh, if that's the way you feel! You need more tact, my friend. [*Insolently*] I want to ask you a question before you go! Are you really willing to admit that you descended from a monkey?

MCINTYRE. Yes, sir, apparently I began where you left off. [*He turns his back on him.*]

BAILEY [*Quite unruffled*]. Then I'll see you at noon, Henry. [*He goes out.*]

SORRELL. Joe's a good fellow when you get to know him. You musn't take everything he says to heart.

MCINTYRE. If you don't mind, I'll go now.

RUTLEDGE. A moment more, my friend. You are leaving us in great bitterness. I am sorry to see that. Can't we be friends? [*McIntyre makes no answer.*]

RUTLEDGE. Has your successor arrived?

MCINTYRE. Yes.

RUTLEDGE. What do you think of him?

MCINTYRE [*With a bitter smile*]. I think they have the man they want.

RUTLEDGE [*Laughing*]. Oh, come, he's not as bad as that, is he?

MCINTYRE. He will teach round or flat, as required, and listen to reason, as they call it. You know the youth must be protected.

RUTLEDGE. Man, man. I admire your courage, but why couldn't you give in a little? You're no longer a young man, McIntyre.

MCINTYRE. I'm younger today than I've been in many a year.

RUTLEDGE. I can hardly believe that, McIntyre. You liked this town and your work here.

MCINTYRE. Yes, as the swine liked Circe.

SORRELL. You know that's a bit radical, Professor. Of course, the people here are a bit conservative.

MCINTYRE. There is no conservative. There is no radical. There's only barbarism and civilization.

RUTLEDGE. And we're barbarians, I suppose?

MCINTYRE. Yes, with your automobiles and your hotels, and your miles of paved streets, I know the whole story of your progress.

RUTLEDGE. Sneer at these things if you will, but I've seen this town grow up from a cross roads village and I've learned to value them. For they stand for something fine and real.

MCINTYRE. Perhaps you have learned to put a value on these things, but I'll never give in to them. Never.

RUTLEDGE. Think a moment, man. You're well fixed here. Even now I could make them take you back.

MCINTYRE. There is no honor in staying.

RUTLEDGE. No, but there's a living, and you've a family. Have you not had honor enough? You wiped the floor with the Baptist minister in the debate.

MCINTYRE. And then the howling pack rushed in.

RUTLEDGE. What of that? You had been too extreme.

MCINTYRE. The truth is always extreme.

RUTLEDGE. If you had only said that evolution was a fact which applied to plants and animals—not to man. I told them I was sure that was your meaning. And then you denied it, condemned everything; accused society; and used the hammer right and left. Why?

MCINTYRE. Because the whole thing is rotten.

RUTLEDGE. Have you anything better to offer?

MCINTYRE. Yes.

RUTLEDGE. What is it?

MCINTYRE. Revolt! Red Revolt! [*Rutledge now shows anger for the first time.*]

RUTLEDGE. If you think that, you are a fool, and a dangerous one.

MCINTYRE. Should I look to you for agreement; you who are so comfortably fixed in the established order? You know nothing of what it means.

RUTLEDGE. Revolt! Revolt! You tell me I know nothing about it! By God, sir, I had drunk the dregs of rebellion before you were out of the cradle. Revolt! What do you reading and writing folks know about these things? Is it you who gets the bullet through the brain, is it you who takes the sword thrust through the bowels? Have you seen your country pillaged and sacked and delivered into the hands of scoundrels; your legislatures corrupted and controlled by darkies; your wealth stolen or destroyed? If you haven't, don't talk to me of revolt. The world may be as bad as you have said, but the biggest rascals of the lot are those who cry 'Revolt'!

MCINTYRE. Much may be said upon both sides.

RUTLEDGE. You were right! There can be no ground between us. You have failed here. So, too, will you fail and be beaten wherever you go.

MCINTYRE. Yet, somehow Rutledge, men have a way of failing and being beaten and presently it appears that those things for which they were defeated have come to pass. [*He goes out.*]

RUTLEDGE. There goes a priceless fool!

SORRELL [*Ever a mediator*]. A good fellow in many ways, but a bit extreme in his views. [*He runs to the door*] Oh, Professor, you mustn't forget your old friends. You must come back and see us some time.

MCINTYRE [*His voice faint and broken down the corridor*]. I'll never come back and see you—Never!

SORRELL [*Returning and shrugging his shoulders*]. Well! It's too bad he feels that way. He always was stubborn.

RUTLEDGE. And now he can eat his heart out,—but his honor is saved.

[*At this moment the negro* JOHNSON *enters. He is about forty years old, of good height, and strong physique, though somewhat paunchy. He wears good dark clothes that fit well, and a derby hat. His features are broad, heavy, but intelligent; his chin is adorned by a silky goatee. He bears himself with considerable dignity which at times verges slightly on pomposity. His language is fairly good, though idiomatic; but the tone of his voice is much the same as that of any other negro.*]

SORRELL. Good morning, Johnson. We've been expecting you. You've never met Mr. Rutledge, have you?

JOHNSON. No, sah, not to mah knowledge.

RUTLEDGE. Well, Johnson, I've wanted to know you for a long time. Give me your hand. [*He shakes the negro's hand.*] I hear nothing but good reports of you.

JOHNSON [*Showing his pleasure*]. Sho'! Who told you all that?

RUTLEDGE [*Waving a hand*]. Everybody, Johnson. They say you're doing fine work down there.

JOHNSON. Oh I keep busy, suh, but I guess I'm out like everyone, fo' the dollah. Niggahs don't pay the doctah so long as they got somethin' else to spend their money on.

RUTLEDGE. But you're doing well, I hear.

JOHNSON. I can't complain. I make a living.

RUTLEDGE. Well then, sit down. [*The negro hesitates.*] That's all right. This is business. [*To Sorrell*] You needn't stay. I'll call you when I need you. [SORRELL *goes into the inner office.*] How long have you lived here, Johnson?

JOHNSON. Off an' on, all my life. I was bawn heah, you know.

RUTLEDGE. Yes, I knew that. You have a family, haven't you?

JOHNSON. A wife and a girl. My other folks is dead. You've seen me aroun', Mistah Rutledge. I used to do odd jobs at yo' house when I was a boy.

RUTLEDGE. Quite likely I have and have forgotten.

JOHNSON. You may have seen my mothah, ole Carrie Johnson. A big black woman, you know?

RUTLEDGE. Yes, I remember her.

JOHNSON. Then, I reckon you know what kind she was?

RUTLEDGE [*Sharply*]. Hush, man! That's no way to talk about your mother.

JOHNSON. It's true, ain't it? I'm not likely to forget it either, so long as othah folks remembers.

RUTLEDGE. What you were, and where you came from matters nothing in this great land of ours. It's what you are that counts.

JOHNSON [*grinning broadly*]. Sho', Mistah Rutledge, I reckon we knows better than that.

RUTLEDGE. If you're the man you are, you deserve all the credit for it.

JOHNSON. I reckon that's right. Nobody but Jim Johnson put me where I am. I tell you, suh, I've been ovah the bumps in my time.

RUTLEDGE. We have that in common, Johnson. Now I suppose you know why I've sent for you.

JOHNSON [*Evasively*]. No, suh.

RUTLEDGE. You've heard of the plan for the new Development, haven't you?

JOHNSON [*Reflectively*]. It does seem I heard something or other about it.

RUTLEDGE. Johnson, we know you to be a progressive citizen who has the best interests of the town at heart. We know you are not the man to stop the wheels of progress. At this crucial hour in our history it is the part of the good citizens of both races to put their shoulders to the wheel.

JOHNSON. What do you want me to do, suh?

RUTLEDGE. The negro settlement as it now stands is a blot on the face of the earth. We want you to help us wipe out that blot and to make that section clean and beautiful.

JOHNSON. I'll do my part if I can.

RUTLEDGE. You can do your part, Johnson, by selling us the house you live in.

JOHNSON. I thought that was comin'.

RUTLEDGE. How long have you owned that house, Johnson?

JOHNSON. Goin' on five years, now.

RUTLEDGE. You bought it from that old man who ran a sanatorium, didn't you?

JOHNSON [*Nodding*]. That's right, sah.

RUTLEDGE. Will you tell me what you paid for the place?

JOHNSON. I paid seventy-five hundred dollars, sah.

RUTLEDGE. Johnson, I'll double that, and pay you cash in hand. That's a big price for that place where it is.

JOHNSON. I don't want to sell, Mistah Rutledge.

RUTLEDGE. Why?

JOHNSON. That house gives me a name. I'm a man who holds his head high.

RUTLEDGE [*Controlling his temper*]. You'll never get a better offer. There aren't many men of your race that can write that big a check.

JOHNSON. No, sah, I reckon not.

RUTLEDGE. You can hold me up if you want, Johnson, but I thought you were too much of a man for that. Go on then, and name your price.

JOHNSON [*Doggedly*]. I've got no price.

RUTLEDGE [*Sternly*]. See here, Johnson, what's the meaning of this?

JOHNSON. I don't want to sell. Ain't that plain enough?

RUTLEDGE. No, it's not. You want to keep on living here, don't you?

JOHNSON [*Rather insolently*]. I sho' does! An' I'm goin' to. I'm goin' to keep right on livin' where I am!

RUTLEDGE. It behooves you to act as a good citizen should, and you're not doing that. You have the respect of the community now. If they find you're holding us back in our efforts to improve and better this town, of which we are both citizens, they will bear only contempt for you.

JOHNSON. Well, what if they do? I'm my own boss, ain't I?

RUTLEDGE. You can't go against public opinion in that head-strong fashion, Johnson.

JOHNSON. I got along without 'em when I was down; I reckon I can get along without 'em when I am up.

RUTLEDGE. That's wild and foolish talk from a man of your race. You're living in a white man's town and you must try to get along with the white man. Besides, I appeal to your civic pride.

JOHNSON. You needn't waste yo' breath, Mistah Rutledge, I'm not going to be forced into anything.

RUTLEDGE. Nobody is trying to force you, Johnson. The day for that is over. But you must learn to obey the white man's law which is the greatest good for the greatest number.

JOHNSON. What's the white man done fo' me, Mistah Rutledge? What's he done fo' me, I say. Nothin'—Nothin' except to give me this yellow skin.

RUTLEDGE [*Sternly*]. That yellow skin has made you what you are, and don't you forget it. But that's enough of that.

JOHNSON. No, they won't talk of it. But it's there just the same. It's there, all right, an' I'm just a nigger to them like the rest. An' I ain't even a niggah to those othahs.

RUTLEDGE. That's enough I say.

JOHNSON. No, it's not. I'm started now, an' I ain't goin' to shut up till I've had my say. Who do you think I am? I'm no common niggah to be bossed around whenever the white man cracks his whip, I hold my head up like any white man, a sight mo' than some white folks I know.

RUTLEDGE [*His patience surely tried, and the lines around his mouth a little tighter*]. That's all very well, but I'm not talking to you about your status in society. Keep to the subject, This is *business*.

JOHNSON [*With a scornful grin*]. Is it? All right! You want to buy my house. I don't want to sell it. That's business, too, an' it's all settled.

RUTLEDGE [*Quietly*] Get out of this office.

JOHNSON [*Leaning over the table*]. Progress, is it? Well, if you want progress, look at me. I was bawn in a shack at the foot o' the hill, an' I've gone to the top where white folks used to live. Ain't that progress enough for you?

RUTLEDGE [*Half rising*]. You black scoundrel, you—

JOHNSON. You ain't foolin' no one. I know why you want that house. But you ain't goin' to get it.

RUTLEDGE [*Gets to his feet and grasps a heavy iron ruler in his hand; his voice is hoarse with passion*]. Get out! You dirty nigger. [SORRELL *rushes in.*] Get out, I say, or I'll kill you! [*The negro goes out with a little taunting smile on his face.*]

SORRELL [*Panting with excitement*]. I was afraid of this! He can't hold out, Mr. Rutledge, he can't! We'll put the screws on now.

RUTLEDGE [*In loathing and despair*]. My God. Is this what white men fought for?

SORRELL [*Grimly*]. We'll get him yet!

RUTLEDGE. My father owned *slaves*. Sorrell! Think of that!

[*But* SORRELL *is thinking of the man who went out the door.*]

Curtain

A lounge and smoking room for men at the Altamont Country Club on a night two weeks later. The room is floored with red tile; the walls are hung with various sporting prints of English gentlemen out fox-hunting—what Oscar Wilde has called "The unspeakable in pursuit of the uneatable."

The walls are panelled with oak halfway up. There are comfortable wall seats around the sides of the room, several deep, heavily cushioned chairs, and in the center, a circular divan.

On this divan, half sitting, half lolling, in correct evening dress, and somewhat conscious of it, with broad and red face shining, and hair plastered smoothly down, is MR. JOSEPH BAILEY, *the Board of Trade Secretary. He is smoking a good fat looking cigar, and smacks his lips greedily around it, playing with it, pushing it hither and yon from one corner of his mouth to another, and licking it. From a distance comes at intervals the strains of brisk dance music.*

Presently SORRELL *comes in with two guests,* PROFESSOR HUTCHINGS, *head of the Department of Social Welfare at the State University, and the politician,* PRESTON CARR, *the governor-elect of the State.* HUTCHINGS *is a small, dapper looking man in his fifties, very brisk and polished in his manner of speech, and proud of the fact that he is, as he is often told, more like a business man than a professor.* PRESTON CARR *is a big, rather vulgar, Saxon type, blond haired. He is somewhat young to be almost a governor; he is a little over forty. Yet this is not surprising, since he began his campaign over twenty years before while a student at the University and has pushed, pushed, pushed, ever since. He is a hand-shaker, a back-slapper, a true exponent of shirtsleeve democracy, for he knows*

every farmer in his native county by first name. To these redoubt-
able gifts he adds an absolute and unscrupulous will to get what he
wants most; he will ponder, bargain, compromise and cheat, and
never lose the smile from his face, never lose the hearty geniality of
his big voice, unless, in a moment of righteous indignation, he flays
a political opponent in the Republican Party, and hints delicately
that he has a tincture of negro blood in his veins, a pleasant device
that never fails to win results. He is what is sometimes called a man
of the people, and our first reflection is that it probably serves them
right.

A firm confidence in the Star of his Destiny, and an unshakable
belief that history is written to prove the infallability of the Demo-
cratic party, "A large easy swallow," in all matters of party doc-
trine, have combined to give him all the self-assurance we can rea-
sonably expect from the union of such qualities as he possesses.
SORRELL *alone is in evening clothes.* PROFESSOR HUTCHINGS *is*
dressed well and quietly in what his tailor called a "three button
sack for business men." PRESTON CARR *wears the uniform of his*
profession: a cut-away, and a white vest with a heavy gold chain
and an elk's tooth charm. All the men are smoking cigars.

SORRELL [*As they enter*]. Oh, hello, Joe, I didn't know you
    were here.
BAILEY. Yes, my wife is a hostess at the dance, you know. [*He*
    gets up and advances toward PRESTON CARR.] Sir, we've
    never met, but I don't feel the need of an introduction to
    the next governor of the State. I'm glad to know you sir.
    I'm a Carr man and a Carr booster. [*Both men shake hands*
    warmly.]
CARR. I knew that when I saw you, I could pick a Carr man
    out of a crowd.
    [PRESTON CARR *has an easy informality in his tone and man-*
    ner that is very reassuring to those who stand in awe of great-
    ness. However, this doesn't include Bailey.]

BAILEY. The State is looking forward to a great era of prosperity and progress, under your administration, Governor.

CARR. Now, that's very good of you, but I'm not elected yet, you know.

BAILEY. A mere matter of form, sir. I often wonder why the Republicans keep sending their men to the polls.

SORRELL. This is Joseph Bailey, Governor.

CARR. What! Not *the* Joseph Bailey. [*Pumps him warmly.*] My dear sir, this is a pleasure. I want to thank you for your splendid work in the primaries.

BAILEY [*Waving his hand*]. Oh, not at all, Governor. We know the right man when we see him. We wanted a young man and a progressive man and we have him. When I read of that first campaign speech, with your wonderful slogan—just how does it go?—[*Pauses*]

CARR. "Life and life more abundant for the people of this State."

BAILEY. "Life and life more abundant for the people of this State." Wonderful! When I saw that I knew we had the man we wanted—a man with *vision*.

CARR [*Bowing*]. I thank you. Do you know I believe that slogan elected me? People cheered it to the very echo.

BAILEY. And no wonder. That's what I call a real constructive program. "Life and life more abundant." It appeals to the imagination. It shows you are alive to the higher spiritual values. It proves—

[SORRELL *who has been trying to gain his attention, now interrupts.*]

SORRELL. Put on the brakes a minute, Joe, and meet Professor Hutchings of the University. [*To the group.*] Joe's a great talker!

BAILEY. What! Is this Professor Hutchings of the Department of Social Service?

HUTCHINGS. It is, sir, and I know you, too. I scarcely feel we require an introduction.

BAILEY [*They shake hands*]. I have long wanted to know the man who edits the University News Dispatch. Your facts and figures about the wealth of the State have been an eye-opener to us all. In fact, sir, I believe every constructive program for the last four years can be tracked down to the Dispatch.

PROFESSOR H. [*Modestly*]. Oh, we have done our small part, but the success of our program was made possible only by such progressive citizens as yourself and the governor, who have put their shoulders to the wheel.

CARR [*Getting the center of the group*]. There is a new spirit alive in this state today. We have done great things; we will do greater. We are looking forward—not backward.

PROFESSOR H. Once the people realize their wealth there is no stopping their progress. The State is a mighty empire, self-sufficient and self-supporting. We are yet, so to speak, pioneer territory. Our potential wealth has hardly been scratched.

CARR. The interesting thing to me, Professor, is how the whole new movement has started in the University.

PROFESSOR H. Yet, don't you think that is the logical starting place for such a movement?

CARR. Beyond a doubt. The growth of the University to meet the new demands of service and leadership is the most gratifying indication of all. What a change since I was a student here!

PROFESSOR H. Yes, there has been a great change, which has marked the passing away of fossilism and old-fogyism. The University is *alive* to its responsibilities; it looks upon itself as an incubator for the future leadership of the State.

CARR. That's it exactly. Take the change, for instance, in the kind of men who are now teaching at the University. Take yourself, Professor. I know of no better illustration. [*The* PROFESSOR *bows slightly.*]

They are men who are alive to what is going on outside. They take an interest in politics and in the party. They go outside and meet the people. They give public addresses. They act as if they were not living for teaching alone. Why, when I was a student, the old fellow who taught me Greek acted as if nothing else in the world mattered.

PROFESSOR H. [*With a laugh*]. Oh, you mean old Billy Bateson.

CARR [*Incredulously*]. You don't mean to tell me he's still living?

PROFESSOR H. Oh yes, he's pensioned off on the Martin fund.

CARR. It's strange how they pop up! I thought surely the old man would be dead by this time.

PROFESSOR H. Oh, no, he still putters around the house and tends his flowers. He hardly ever comes out, however. A nice old fellow, you know, but utterly behind the times. We saw he was absolutely unable to grasp the larger significance of things so we eased him off.

SORRELL. It's just as well you did, I think. I know when I was in school they tried to get me to take all that stuff, but I couldn't see it that way. I was telling a man a week or so back that I thought the whole thing was a mistake.

BAILEY. Still, there's something to be said for this culture. When a man comes home at night, tired and worn out from his day's work, it's a great thing to be able to pick up a good book, and so to speak, rest his mind.

PROFESSOR H. Oh, undoubtedly, there's a great recreational value in the fine arts. We have recognized that in the School of Business Administration and we compel all our freshmen to take a course in the Fine Arts.

CARR. That strikes me as a very sensible and practical idea. A man should be rounded out, as it were. [*He makes an expansive gesture.*]

PROFESSOR H. Yes, we thought so too. So for *two* hours a week we give our men a course which grounds them in the fundamentals of art, comparative literature, and the modern drama. The engineering school is doing somewhat the same thing for its men in its class of engineering English.

BAILEY. Splendid! Fifteen minutes a day works wonders, I am told.

SORRELL. Of course, a man ought not to be one-sided.

PROFESSOR H. I consider that the great advance that has been made in modern education is the relating of it to everyday life. Fifty years ago we thought education was something intended exclusively for the use of gentlemen and the sons of gentlemen. That has all changed. The common man has come forward and asserted his rights. He has insisted that education should first of all be useful.

CARR. And rightly so,—what other purpose could it serve?

PROFESSOR H. The average citizen of this state is a shrewd, hard-headed, practical fellow, with a strong infusion of Scotch blood, who first of all wants the facts. "What good is all this education to me or my children?" he says. That was the problem the University had to face a few years ago, and we knew we had to meet the issue with facts, not with beautiful phrases. So it has been part of my work on the News Dispatch to point out to the good people of this state the practical value of training at the University, the dollars and cents advantage, to put it plainly.

BAILEY. I've always said you could rely on the common sense of our people.

CARR. What could better illustrate the infallible instinct of the common people for knowing the right thing, and getting it? If I understand you, this whole great educational reform originated among the masses of the people?

PROFESSOR H. Yes, sir, it amounts to that.

CARR. It is another triumph, and a notable one, for democratic institutions.

SORRELL. I never had a chance to go to college and there's not a day of my life that I don't regret it. I got my education in the University of Hard Knocks and what I've done, I've done myself.

CARR. You have no reason to apologize for that, my friend.

SORRELL. Oh, I've done well enough, but I keep thinking how much better I could've done if I'd had the chance some fellows have. I was telling my boy the other day a man simply couldn't afford to do without a college course in this day and time. The competition's getting too stiff.

PROFESSOR H. That spirit is evident now all over the State. We have made the people alive to the necessity of the educational program just as a few years ago we made them see the necessity of the good roads program. Last year our appropriations to State institutions were greater than those of any other southern state. This year we will do still better, if I know the Governor here.

CARR. You know your man. I'm for you, tooth and nail.

BAILEY. That's the great thing about our people; when they see a thing needs doing, they do it.

SORRELL. I read somewhere the other day where some fellow lately has said the South has no literature, no art, no culture of any kind. He called it "the Sahara of the Bozart," or something of the sort.

CARR [Hotly]. That's a damnable libel! I read it too. I wouldn't be surprised if the man is a Republican. They never lose a chance to blacken our name. [Violently.] I tell you there's nothing to which those fellows won't stoop.

PROFESSOR H. Now that I think of it, I read the article too. It's made quite a stir. I think we can answer him by producing the facts. [He takes a folded slip of paper from a notebook.] I looked up the facts in the matter, and they are as follows: Irvin S. Nasby who has so many articles in the Saturday Evening Post, himself a Southerner and a noted humorist, is authority for the statement that the South has proportionately more literary men than any other part of the country.

CARR [*Triumphantly*]. Listen to that! I knew it!

PROFESSOR H. As for the past, let these names speak for themselves and then judge whether we have anything to be ashamed of. [*Reads*] In poetry, Edgar Allan Poe and Sidney Lanier.

CARR. Names to conjure with!

BAILEY. We have their works at home.

PROFESSOR H. [*Reading*]. As well as numerous other famous names, a few of which I will read you: Willard Pettigrew, whose Rhymes of the Cotton Belt are known everywhere; Henry S. Tillingsworth, who wrote the Razorback Lyrics; Ephraim Doolittle, who early gained fame as the author of Pearls of the Piedmont; Dinwiddie Stuart, who carved his way to glory with his immortal "Ode to the F.F.V.'s" and many others, whose names I will not mention here.

SORRELL [*Who has been counting on his fingers*]. That makes six in poetry.

HUTCHINGS [*Proceeding*]. In prose, it is only necessary to mention the names of Joel Chandler Harris, whose Uncle Remus stories are dear to the hearts of children of all ages, the immortal O'Henry, Edgar Allan Poe, Sidney Lanier, Augusta J. Evans, Thomas Nelson Page, John Fox, Jr.; William Gilmore Simms, Charles Egbert Craddock, Sophonisba Stevens, Jefferson Giddings, Jackson T. Busbee, and Eleazer Martin.

BAILEY. All well-known names.

CARR. How many does that make, Sorrell?

SORRELL. Thirteen in prose.

CARR. Give us another name, my dear Professor.

PROFESSOR H. Then I need only mention Philip Fuller, whose

travel book, "Afoot in the Everglades," is known wherever the English language is spoken.

SORRELL. That makes fourteen in prose.

CARR. A record of which every true-born Southerner may be proud.

PROFESSOR H. That makes a total of twenty authors, all of whom are dead.

BAILEY [*Triumphantly*]. Did you hear that? They are all dead!

CARR [*Solemnly*]. Their place in literature is imperishably fixed.

PROFESSOR H. Yes, sir. And it may interest you to know, Governor, that all of them voted the Democratic ticket.

CARR. A splendid record! And it shows plainly the reason for the libelous and defamatory accusations that have been made. Manifestly, it is another Republican trick.

SORRELL. Still it seems to me it's up to all of us to do all we can for culture. You've got to sell people the idea; put the whole thing on a business basis. Why can't other towns in the State show the same spirit as Altamont? We're making a yearly event now of the music festival in August.

CARR. That is splendid.

SORRELL. Yes, and it's practical, too. We had to guarantee the Philadelphia Symphony twenty thousand dollars to get them here for a week this summer, but we never lost a cent. The Rotary Club had underwritten the whole amount in fifteen minutes. We estimated that the festival brought two thousand new visitors to town that week, who spent on an average fifty dollars each. Total: One hundred thousand dollars.

BAILEY. To say nothing of the splendid advertising! Every one of those people went away and told their friends. Next summer four thousand will come instead of two thousand. The summer after, eight thousand. Wait a minute! [*He figures rapidly on a piece of paper.*]

SORRELL. What are you doing?

BAILEY. I'm trying to estimate the number in 1930.

SORRELL. We've got our own music now, and we've put it on a paying basis. Why can't we do the same for our own literature?

PROFESSOR H. There's no reason in the world why we shouldn't. It's all a matter of initiative and organization, and we have that in marked degree.

CARR [*In measured platform speech*]. We should, we ought, we must foster a native literature if only to repudiate the vicious slurs of our enemies. The soil of our glorious Southland is fairly teeming with native and original geniuses who only await the sympathetic encouragement of the State, and the party, to produce immortal masterpieces.

PROFESSOR H. It is all a matter of energy, rightly applied. I never tire of quoting a saying of the great Thomas A. Edison: "Genius is one tenth inspiration and nine-tenths perspiration." We excel in genius of that order. The same spirit that has expressed itself in carving roads through the rock of mountain passes, the genius that has expressed itself in statesmanship, in building up a great school system, may express itself in any given direction.

CARR. I concur in all you have said, Professor. It should be the part of all serious-minded people, of business man, farmer, and statesman, to let our young writers know we are now willing to recognize the refining influence of literary endeavor. We have made ourselves a good stout pair of boots, so to speak, and we are wearing them. It is entirely fitting and proper we *should* now see them get polished. The Democratic party has always been alive to the progressive issues of the moment, and it will not prove retrograde to its duty now.

SORRELL. You have hit the nail on the head, Governor. We

should encourage our young writers and make it worth their while to stay at home. We have plenty of local talent, but so much of it goes north.

BAILEY. Yes; there is that Powell boy, for example. But there is one thing he said that bothers me: that he didn't think the South could have a serious literature at the present time that didn't deal in some way with the negro question.

SORRELL. Oh, oh.

PROFESSOR H. [*Coughing dryly*]. The young man evidently needs a little mental discipline—if I may say so, social discipline.

CARR. True! True! These are tender subjects, very tender subjects. Of course, we're all for artistic liberty.

BAILEY. Oh, of course.

CARR. But within bounds, within reasonable bounds. We mustn't inflame dangerous issues by airing them.

PROFESSOR H. Absolutely not. We must not go beyond the bounds of public decency.

CARR. I agree with you; we must point out the advantages of living here, and reclaim these wanderers to the field, so to speak.

[*The men, one by one, begin to toss away their cigars, preparatory to quitting the room.*]

BAILEY. There's no reason why Altamont should not be the logical place for a great artistic colony: water, scenery, climate,—all point to it as an artistic center. [*They move in pairs toward the door.*]

PROFESSOR H. These things we need and they will come in their proper order. We are well embarked on our road program, enormous strides are being made in the educational system; we are building up a great industrial state:— soon our cotton mills will outnumber those of New England. These things are necessary and must come if we are to keep abreast of the times. After that—

SORRELL. Shall we go out now?

CARR. We might as well, I suppose—you were saying, Professor—?

PROFESSOR H. [*In hard, precise tones*]. After that, I said, we will give the poets a chance. [*They pause at the door.*]

CARR [*Gallantly*]. After you, Professor.

PROFESSOR H. [*Ditto*]. You first, my dear Governor. Everything, you know, in its proper order. [*So they go out in this order, with* SORRELL *and* BAILEY *behind.*]

BAILEY [*With enthusiasm*]. A very stimulating talk! The Governor is a fine man, isn't he? He's so plain and simple in his ways.

SORRELL. Oh, the Governor is the simplest of men—by the way, have you heard the news; the nigger Johnson has come across. He'll sign the deeds tomorrow.

BAILEY. That's great business! Now things will move! I knew he couldn't stand the pressure. The old man is tickled, I'll bet.

[LEE RUTLEDGE, *wearing a dinner jacket, enters the room.*]

BAILEY. Hello, Lee!

LEE. Hello!

BAILEY. You'll be going back soon, won't you?

LEE. Yes,—tomorrow.

SORRELL. I hope you'll come in and see us before you go, Lee.

LEE. Thanks. I will if I have time.

BAILEY. I'll say good-bye now. We're expecting big things of you, Lee. Your father's record gives you something to shoot at. Good luck to you, son.

LEE. Thank you, Mr. Bailey. The same to you. Good-bye! [*He shakes hands with* BAILEY, *and the two men go out.* LEE *produces a cigarette and lights it. He smokes rapidly, and nervously fidgets around, as if impelled by some restless and indefinable desire. Presently* "BULL" PATTON, *a hulking, coarsely*

*handsome young man of twenty-two enters the room. He also is
wearing a dinner jacket.*]

LEE. Hello, Bull.

BULL. Hello. Give me a light, will you. [LEE *does so.* "BULL"
lights a cigarette.]

LEE. Stagging it?

BULL. Yes. Are you?

LEE. Yes. [*They smoke in silence a moment.*]

LEE. Rotten dance, isn't it?

BULL. Rotten is right!

LEE. Like the music?

BULL. Rotten! And the girls!

LEE. Rotten!

BULL. Where have all the *good* girls gone to, Lee?

LEE. The *good girls*?

BULL. Well, you know what I mean.

LEE. Most of 'em have gone back to school. And most of the
summer girls are gone, too.

BULL. When are you going back?

LEE. Tomorrow. When are you?

BULL. Oh, in a day or so, I guess.

LEE. You don't seem to be in a hurry.

BULL. I'm not.

LEE. I thought you had a good chance to make the team this
year.

BULL [*Gloomily*]. No. I'm not eligible.

LEE. Didn't pass enough work? [BULL *nods.*] Tough luck!

BULL. I don't much want to go back, Lee, but the old man
says I've got to. He's starting me in the Business Course
this year. I've tried about everything else.

LEE. How long have you been going off to school?

BULL. Third college, fifth year.

LEE. Great God! [*They both laugh loudly.*]

BULL. What's the use, Lee? Why don't they leave me alone?

I'll never get through. I'm not that kind. But you know
how it is. Get an education, get an education! Everyone's
crazy on the subject. Well, damn it, Lee. I don't want an
education. I'm not that kind. I couldn't get it if I tried.
You can't go out and buy it by the square yard, can you?

LEE. Well, everyone says you can't get ahead without one today, so it must be so.

BULL. Ah, the hell it is.

[*A young man, pasty faced, sharp featured, and rather heavily
inebriated, reels into the room with a fixed leer on his face.*]

LEE. Doggy, I'm surprised at you.

DOGGY [*Coming close and whispering hoarsely*]. Say Lee, d'ye
know I'm—hic—drunk?

LEE [*In tones of disbelief*]. No?

DOGGY [*Solemnly wagging his head*]. Yes,—hic—I am, too.

BULL. Go on Doggy, you know you're not.

LEE. We don't believe you.

DOGGY. Yes—hic—I am [*he leers slyly*]—an' I'm goin' to get
still drunker.

[*He goes out.*]

BULL. Did *he* bring anyone tonight?

LEE. Yes, he's with Mary Todd Wheeler.

BULL. Isn't her mother a hostess?

LEE. Yes.

BULL. Oh, well, it wouldn't matter. Mrs. Wheeler would just
love Doggy's money, wouldn't she?

LEE. I think that's the idea. [BULL *looks at his watch.*]

LEE. Almost time for the intermission, isn't it?

BULL. Yes, have you your car here?

LEE. Yes, why?

BULL. I thought we might get a couple of 'em out, maybe.

LEE. What for?

BULL. Oh, we might get a little neck.

LEE. With that bunch! Why, most of them were going to

dances when Sherman marched through Georgia. Besides, they're all dated up with the fellows who brought em.

BULL. This is a wild little town, isn't it?

LEE. Yes, when you know it from the inside.

BULL. I wonder if we're bad, or if people were always like this. The old man says we're no worse than they used to be.

LEE. I'd hate to think it.

BULL. So would I. [*Pause*] Say, there's one hot-looking girl on the floor tonight.

LEE. Pink dress?

BULL. Yes. Did you notice her?

LEE. Did I!

BULL. Who is she?

LEE. I don't know. They call her Bobby. She's visiting Mary Todd Wheeler.

BULL. Some shape on her, hasn't she?

LEE. She's *built*, all right.

BULL. Where's she from?

LEE. Atlanta.

BULL. Oh! oh! that settles it for me. I'm going around to see *that* lady.

LEE. You'll have to get in line then. There's a list a foot long.

BULL. She must be a neck-artist.

LEE. You see right into things, don't you?

[*They are silent, but smoke nervously and move restlessly for a moment.*]

LEE [*Getting up suddenly*]. Oh, damn it, let's go somewhere.

BULL. Go where?

LEE. I don't know; anywhere. I want to do something: I don't know what it is. I get wild like this every year before I go back.

BULL. Same here. Can you take your car?

LEE. Yes.

[*A girl, dressed very prettily, in a blue silk dress, comes by the door, pauses in the opening, and gazes quickly and furtively over her shoulder.*]

LEE. Hello, Mary Todd.

MARY TODD [*With a start*]. Oh, hello, Lee. Why aren't you dancing?

LEE. Fed up, I guess.

BULL. Hello, Mary Todd.

MARY TODD. I didn't see you, Bull.

LEE. Who's that good-looking girl staying at your house? Bull wants to know her.

MARY TODD. That's Bobby Andrews. *Isn't* she pretty? We were in school together.

LEE [*With a formal bow*]. That accounts for it, then.

BULL. Fix me up a date with her, can't you? I want to meet her.

MARY TODD. When?

BULL [*Hopefully*]. What about the intermission?

MARY TODD. You don't want much, do you? You'll have to get in line and take your chance, Bull. She's getting an awful rush.

BULL. Well, when can you fix it for me?

MARY TODD. Next week, sometime. Maybe.

BULL. Oh, lord! I'll have gone then.

MARY TODD. I'm afraid that's the best I can do.

BULL. This is a rotten town and a rotten dance.

MARY TODD. Give me a cigarette, Lee. I'm sneaking out to smoke and to get away from Doggy. [LEE *gives her cigarettes*].

LEE. Doggy's pretty far gone. Isn't he?

MARY TODD. He's perfectly disgusting. I've had to practically hold him up all night. Doggy's perfectly killing when he's had one or two drinks, but I don't like to see a boy get like this, do you?

LEE. No, it's bad on the eyes.

MARY TODD. If you see mama and she asks for me, don't tell her where I am.

[*She goes out.*]

BULL [*Getting up*]. Well, let's go! I want to do something. There's nothing doing here. [*They put on their hats and light overcoats.*]

LEE. I wonder if Mary Todd's mother has seen Doggy.

BULL. Of course she has. They all came together.

LEE. The old lady must be blind in both eyes.

BULL. Not on your life!

LEE. But, good Lord, you saw him when he was in here, didn't you?

BULL. It's not what you see that counts; it's what you pretend not to see.

LEE [*Passionately*]. By God! It's too common! It's like a public market! I'm sick of it! Let's get out! [MRS. WHEELER, *a portly, beaming matron, in a glittering black dress comes by. She has a fat, throaty voice, and a carved smile of frozen amiability which cannot wholly conceal, however, her cold little eyes, and her underlying hardness.*]

MRS. WHEELER. Oh—good evening, Lee.

LEE [*Respectfully*]. Good evening, Mrs. Wheeler.

MRS. WHEELER. And how are you, Thomas?

BULL. Pretty well, thank you, Mrs. Wheeler.

MRS. WHEELER. It's a lovely dance, isn't it?

[LEE *says "oh fine" and* BULL *mutters "Yes'm."*]

MRS. WHEELER. I'm looking for my little girl; we must be going home—have you seen her?

LEE. No ma'am. Not lately.

MRS. WHEELER. The child so enjoys these affairs. She was perfectly radiant tonight. It's such a pleasure to me to come and watch her; she's like a little elf. Lee, I do hope you'll come to see us before you go back. Mary Todd is always *so* glad to see her old friends.

LEE. Thank you, Mrs. Wheeler, but I'm afraid I can't. I go back tomorrow.

MRS. WHEELER. Oh! What a pity! Mary Todd will be *so* disappointed. I hoped both you boys would come around. She has the *sweetest* girl friend from Atlanta. Thomas, at least you can come.

BULL [*Faithfully*]. Yes'm, I'll try.

MRS. WHEELER [*Purring softly*]. Good! Mary Todd will be *so* pleased—[*peering down the hall*] I wonder where the child can be. She ran off and left Joseph all alone. [*At this moment* DOGGY *appears, considerably more inebriated than before. The two young men exchange quick, significant looks.* MRS. WHEELER *never changes a muscle of her beaming face.*] Why Joseph, we were just talking about you! [*He leers drunkenly at her and gestures to himself.*]

DOGGY. Talkin' 'bout me?

MRS. WHEELER. Hum! yes—Perhaps she's out on the veranda. [*She moves a few steps away but not out of sight.*]

DOGGY [*To* LEE]. I tol' you I'd get good an' drunk, didn't I?

LEE [*Curtly*]. Yes.

DOGGY [*Leering again and pointing to himself*]. Well-e-e-e- ain' I?

LEE [*Coldly*]. Yes, you are.

BULL [*Impatiently*]. Come on, let's go! [*They go out.*]

LEE and BULL. Good night, Mrs. Wheeler.

MRS. WHEELER. Good night, boys. [*She espies her child.*] Oh, there she is now! [*calls*] Mary To-dd.

MARY TODD [*Down the corridor*]. Yes, Mama.

MRS. WHEELER [*Pleasantly*]. Come dear! Joseph is waiting for you.

MARY TODD [*Down the corridor, a trifle wearily*]. Yes, mama.

[*The inebriated* DOGGY *reels to the corridor opening, and, gripping his hands firmly against the wall, leans far out, peering drunkenly and stupidly down the passageway in the direction from which the girl's voice has come.* MRS. WHEELER, *remarkable lady, beams brightly and inflexibly.*]

Curtain

SCENE **5**

*A room in the home of the negro, Johnson. Lights of the settlement,
smoky and dim, below. Lights of the town, clear and sharp, in the
distance.*

*From below there is the hum of a powerful motor climbing la-
boriously up the unpaved, lumpy street.*

*A mulatto girl, nineteen years old, enters the room, and goes to
the window. She is the daughter of the negro Johnson. She is
dressed cleanly and neatly, and her coarse, black hair, which is
straight, is combed flatly down on either side, and bound in a knot
behind. She is well developed, and has thin, but not sharp features.*

*The automobile stops outside; the motor is throttled to a low
hum. In a moment* LEE RUTLEDGE *crosses the porch and enters the
room. She is somewhat startled by his sudden appearance, but com-
poses herself quickly, although she shows pleasure by a sudden,
swift gleam of her eyes, and a momentary glimpse of white teeth.*

LEE. Hello, Annie.

ANNIE. Hello, Mistah Lee.

[*A pause*]

LEE. I thought I saw you at the window, so I took a chance,
and came in. [*There is a certain unconscious insolence in his
manner. A pause.*] How've you been?

ANNIE. Oh, pretty well. [*A pause*] Where've you been keepin'
yo'self? I haven't seen yo' in a long time.

LEE. Oh, busy mostly. [*An awkward pause. He looks around.*]

ANNIE. What yo' lookin' at?

LEE [*Grinning*]. I'm looking at my house, Annie. How do
you like it? [*A pause*] What've you been doing?

ANNIE. Oh—nothin'. [*A pause*] What's there fo' me to do, anyway? I might as well be in jail as heah.

LEE. Your old man keeps you pinned down pretty close, doesn't he?

[*Dance music,—jazz with a very primitive, a very compelling rhythm is heard, somewhere off in the settlement. It is a little franker, a little more vulgar than the dance music played at dances of white people.*] What's that?

ANNIE. Oh, the niggahs are havin' a dance, I reckon.

LEE. Don't you ever go?

ANNIE [*Scornfully*]. What do yo' think I am? You don't catch me mixin' up with that black trash. [*A pause*] You must've been to a dance yo'self.

LEE. Yes, I have been.

[*The automobile klaxon honks impatiently outside.*]

ANNIE. Who's with you?

LEE. Oh, a friend of mine.

ANNIE. Who is he? Do I know him?

LEE [*Irritably*]. No. He's a friend of *mine*, I told you. You've never seen him.

ANNIE [*Angered*]. How do you know? You don't think you're the only white boy I know, do you?

LEE [*Annoyed*]. Ah, you can't fool me. Where'd you ever get to know any white boys?

ANNIE. Maybe where I got to know you—in the dark.

LEE. Ah, cut it out! [*A pause. Quietly*]. Where is everyone?

ANNIE. Papa's in town. He won't be back till late.

LEE. Where's your mother?

ANNIE. She went to meetin'.

LEE [*Jocosely*]. You haven't gone and got religion, too, have you?

ANNIE. No, an' I'm not goin' to. You don't catch me foolin' with those crazy niggahs, singin' an' shoutin', and prayin' till two o'clock in the mawnin', sometimes.

LEE. You don't go with any of these—people, do you?

ANNIE [*As if stung by the implication*]. I'm no niggah!

LEE [*With rather brutal mockery*]. No? What are you, then? The
Queen of Sheba?

[*Music off-stage*]

ANNIE [*Sullenly*]. Niggahs don't have straight hair like that,
do they? [*She pats her own. A pause*]. I saw you on the
street the other day!

LEE. Did you? [*A pause*] I didn't see you.

ANNIE. Yes you didn't! You turned yo' head when you saw
me comin',—I saw you!

LEE [*Sternly*]. What d'ye take me for? [*A pause*] Yes, I saw
you. Don't you ever speak to me on the street again, Annie. You ought to have sense enough to know better.

ANNIE [*Passionately*]. You're speakin' to me now, ain't yo'?

LEE. Don't be a damn fool!

[*The automobile klaxon honks impatiently again.*]

ANNIE [*With smoldering bitterness*]. Yo' friend mus' be in a
hurry. Go on, if you want to. Some one you know might
see you.

LEE. Don't you want to go with me?

ANNIE. Go wheah?

LEE. Oh—for a little ride,—up the mountain.

ANNIE. If I'm not good enough to speak to, I'm not good
enough to ride with, I reckon.

[*Music off-stage*]

LEE [*Angrily*]. Then go to the nigger dance, if you like; I
won't fool with you any longer.

ANNIE [*With the cry of a wounded animal*]. I don't have to go
with niggahs! I can go with white boys!

LEE. Ah—you're crazy!

[*He turns to go out. The savage rhythm of the dance music is
heard again. The girl's face darkens with pain and disgust. In a
moment she controls herself and speaks quietly, but with a sullen note in her voice.*]

ANNIE. Is yo' friend goin', too?

LEE. Yes. [*A pause*]

ANNIE. I'll get my hat and coat. You'd bettah wait outside.

LEE. That's more like it. We'll be waiting in the car. Make it snappy, won't you?

[*He turns to leave the room, but as he nears the open window, he is blocked suddenly by the bulky body of the negro* JOHNSON *who has crossed the porch quickly and now enters the room, carefully planting himself before the windows. The negro's manner betrays a high degree of emotion and anger. He breathes heavily and it is some moments before he controls himself sufficiently to speak.*]

JOHNSON [*Sternly*]. What're yo' doin' heah, Mistah Lee?

[*The boy is white faced, but at the negro's tone his back stiffens and his head springs up like a lash. He makes no answer. The negro is angry; he grasps the young man roughly by the arm. They come to grips, the boy is fastened in the man's powerful arms, and in the struggle, his soft, felt hat is knocked off.*]

LEE [*Furiously*]. Take your hands off me, you damn nigger!

[*He strikes the negro a heavy blow in the face, which staggers him, and causes him to reel back against the wall. The boy rushes out through the window. The negro recovers himself quickly and follows. The girl runs to her father and clings desperately to his arm, saying nothing. Outside the car leaps off and rushes away down the hill.* JOHNSON *turns to the girl, and removes her grasp forcibly. She retreats under his glare and he advances slowly upon her to the end of the scene.*]

JOHNSON [*His yellow eyes are staring with rage*]. So this is the way you do when my back's tu'ned! I keeps you away from the othah niggahs. I tell my folks to hold theah heads up,—and the minute I get away, yo' make a whore out of yo'self with a white boy!

Curtain

SCENE **6**

The library of the attorney, MR. RUTLEDGE. *The room is a high,
massive chamber, with beams of quartered oak, and wainscoting.
The furniture is likewise dark and cushioned with leather. Here* MR.
RUTLEDGE *has accumulated a large law library. The books are
racked on both sides of the room in thick, yellow rows. High French
windows at the back open on a broad veranda bordered by a low,
heavy white rail; beyond there is a dark vision of clumped flower
bushes, shrubbery and a spacious lawn. A door between the cases of
books at the left opens to other parts of the house.*

*It is the same night. A clock in town strikes eleven times; the
attorney* RUTLEDGE *is discovered seated at a table in the rear, with
his back to the windows, which are open. He is smoking a big black
pipe, poring intently over a mass of papers on the table. Several
large, calf-skin volumes are open around him.*

*Presently the door opens and his wife comes in. She is a woman
in her late fifties, very much preoccupied with her own interests,
which are many, very sure of their importance, and with little or no
sense of humor. She is really a very pleasant and sweet-natured
lady—not at all like* MRS. WHEELER, *but, to put it plainly, she is
trifling, and no account,—a sort of female Rip Van Winkle, but
with a great show of energy and enthusiasm which she has exhausted rapidly and earnestly on whatever has held the stage of her
fancy from the days of the Montessori method to the more recent
developments of the Drama League, and New Thought. She is a
source of vast entertainment to her husband, who treats her with all
the tenderness, but with all the lack of seriousness, he would dis-
play toward the whimsical caprices of a well-beloved child. Of this
fact she has never been fully aware.*

She is bearing a book in her hand in which are some sheets of paper, on which there is writing. She comes in and sits down by the table.

MRS. RUTLEDGE. May I come in?

RUTLEDGE [*Looking up*]. Yes. Sit down and stay a while.

MRS. RUTLEDGE. Oh dear! I feel a wreck.

RUTLEDGE [*Proceeding with his work*]. So!

MRS. RUTLEDGE. I'll be glad when this week's over.

RUTLEDGE. Busy? [*He works on.*]

MRS. RUTLEDGE. I'm coaching one of the Drama League plays and I must read a paper to the Quill Club, Friday, and I've hardly begun it yet.

RUTLEDGE [*Working on*]. What's—the—subject?

MRS. RUTLEDGE. "The Drama as a Social Force."

RUTLEDGE [*While he works*]. Interesting?

MRS. RUTLEDGE. Very. There's an awfully good article in the encyclopedia. Can you give me some help?

RUTLEDGE. Afraid not—I don't know enough on the subject.

MRS. RUTLEDGE [*Sighing*]. Oh dear! I wish the Riders wasn't taking up so much time.

RUTLEDGE. The what?

MRS. RUTLEDGE. The play I'm coaching: "Riders to the Sea."

RUTLEDGE. Oh! [*He goes on working.*]

MRS. RUTLEDGE. We're putting on two others, too. [*She waits expectantly but he does not answer.*] Lady Gregory's "Rising of the Moon," and Lord Dunsany's "Night at an Inn."

RUTLEDGE. Good. [*He works on.*]

MRS. RUTLEDGE. After that we're going to produce Booth Tarkington's "Clarence" and O'Neill's "Beyond the Horizon."

RUTLEDGE. Splendid. [*He works on.*]

MRS. RUTLEDGE. You don't seem a bit interested, Will.

RUTLEDGE [*Looking up*]. Of course I am.

MRS. RUTLEDGE. At the end of the year we're going to produce three one-act plays written by members of the club. They are to represent the development of the play and the dance in different countries—Ireland, Burma, Spain. I'm writing one of them now.

RUTLEDGE [*Absently*]. Are you, honey?

MRS. RUTLEDGE. Yes, Mrs. Bailey is writing one of them, too. The Burmese thing.

RUTLEDGE. Mrs. Board-of-Trade Bailey?

MRS. RUTLEDGE. Yes, and Mrs. Parsons is writing a perfectly beautiful play about Spain.

RUTLEDGE. Who is Mrs. Parsons?

MRS. RUTLEDGE. Oh, you know her, the dentist's wife.

RUTLEDGE. Dentist's wife? Oh! about Spain, you say?

MRS. RUTLEDGE. Well, the scenes are in Spain, but the characters are from different places. An Italian tenor falls in love with a Russian dancer and marries her; this rouses the jealousy of a Spanish toreador, who loves her, also. There's a thrilling scene at the end where the toreador opens the gate and lets the mad bulls rush over the lovers.

RUTLEDGE. Is any one hurt?

MRS. RUTLEDGE. Hurt? They're both killed; anyway, it's going to be perfectly thrilling.

RUTLEDGE. I should think you'd have trouble making the bulls behave.

MRS. RUTLEDGE. Yes, that is the only difficulty. But the rest of the play goes beautifully—I do hope you'll take more time for these things hereafter, Will. You really ought, you know. Your position in the community demands you show an interest in the finer things of life. Oh, dear. I do wish you weren't so professional. And you have the same views your grandfather had. You know you have.

RUTLEDGE. But if they're good views, honey, why change them?

MRS. RUTLEDGE. Because they're old-fashioned, that's why.

RUTLEDGE. As for instance?

MRS. RUTLEDGE. Well, you think the South can do no wrong.

RUTLEDGE. I never said that, did I?

MRS. RUTLEDGE. Well, you act it.

RUTLEDGE. Do I?

MRS. RUTLEDGE. You think nothing matters which doesn't happen in your own back yard.

RUTLEDGE. My dear, I don't believe for a moment that all roads lead to Rome, but the Romans thought so. And it's really not a bad idea. It gives you a certain firmness, a certain confidence, a certain grasp on things, you can't quite get in any other way.

MRS. RUTLEDGE. Well I don't care. I think it's narrow and provincial. Of course, I believe in being loyal—

RUTLEDGE. To what?

MRS. RUTLEDGE. To our Mother.

RUTLEDGE. Our Mother?

MRS. RUTLEDGE. Yes, you know, someone said, the South was a great Mother to us all.

RUTLEDGE. No, She is not a mother; she is a mistress.

MRS. RUTLEDGE. Will! Have a little decency!

RUTLEDGE. She is a *mighty* mistress: forever young, forever old. She is removed from the world, yet does she contrive to make you feel the world is removed from her. She makes virtues of her prejudices, glorifies her superstitions, and extols her ignorance; she sanctifies the average, and crucifies the unusual: she always was and always will be incapable of seeing more than one side,— her own. But she has sent forth her lovers with plumes in their hats; she has taught them to die without regret, so long as they might die like cavaliers. Passionate, generous, cruel, noble—she is our Queen to whose services

we are bound, in whose service, we shall die! Who
would have her any different?

[RUTLEDGE, *having thus delivered himself, is silent, and stares
straight ahead, with eyes which burn bright and deep. His wife,
who has been held in a kind of awed fascination, now moves
nervously and clears her throat.*]

MRS. RUTLEDGE. Really, dear, I don't think that's very nice.

RUTLEDGE [*With a smile*]. Don't you, honey? Have I shocked
you?

MRS. RUTLEDGE [*Indignantly*]. *Shocked* me! I'm not that easily
shocked. But I think you're living in the past, Will.

RUTLEDGE. Well, yes.

MRS. RUTLEDGE. You don't take us at all seriously?

RUTLEDGE. My dear, you have been a delightful amateur in
one thing and another for twenty years, and I love you
for it. If you became professional, I'd spank you.

MRS. RUTLEDGE [*With a sigh*]. Oh, Will, I wonder if you'll ever
let me grow up?

RUTLEDGE. What for? I think children are most attractive
when they're at your age, honey. [*Looks at his watch.*] It's
eleven thirty.

MRS. RUTLEDGE. I suppose you'll say now I've spoiled your
whole evening's work.

RUTLEDGE. I was almost through, as a matter of fact. I'll have
more time hereafter. That negro came across today. We're
going to finish the business tomorrow.

MRS. RUTLEDGE. Thank heaven for that! Really he acted in a
most ungrateful and insolent manner, after you were so
kind to him.

RUTLEDGE. Oh, that's all over now. I made the mistake of los-
ing my temper. I regret the whole incident very much.
You can hardly blame the fellow,—we went at him so
suddenly.

MRS. RUTLEDGE. But the idea of his saying the things that he did! [*Pause*] What are we going to do with those people, Will?

RUTLEDGE. It begins to look, honey, as if we're going to have to understand them.

MRS. RUTLEDGE. But they're such animals!

RUTLEDGE. Who knows! [*A pause while he stares thoughtfully before him.*] Who knows!

MRS. RUTLEDGE. What's to be done, Will?

[RUTLEDGE *lifts his arms with a little shrug. There is a pause.*]

MRS. RUTLEDGE. Now that you have the old house back, what are you going to do with it?

RUTLEDGE [*Thoughtfully*]. It's strange how the value of a thing goes down the closer you come to it. Now that I almost have it, I wonder if I ever wanted it.

MRS. RUTLEDGE [*Impatiently*]. Of course you did! I have seen you become almost frantic over it. At least, there'll be no more darkies living there now.

RUTLEDGE. No, we'll put an end to that, I was thinking . . .

MRS. RUTLEDGE. What?

RUTLEDGE. That some day, after Lee comes back from college and is married and settled down, I might give the house to him.

MRS. RUTLEDGE. Do you want to go back there yourself?

RUTLEDGE. No, honey, the charm and the bloom have faded for me. I am at that time of life, my dear, when the very notion of change is abhorrent. After all, do houses matter?

MRS. RUTLEDGE. Will, what a way to talk after all your worry!

RUTLEDGE. They do, I suppose. Well, we'll give it to Lee and someday the Rutledge family will be established there again. There's something in tradition, I suppose. [*They are both silent a moment.*] Has Lee returned yet?

MRS. RUTLEDGE. No, but I don't expect him until after midnight. Those dances at the country club often last later than that.

RUTLEDGE. I hoped he would stay home tonight, his last night at home.

MRS. RUTLEDGE. I think it would kill the boy to keep still. He must be doing something constantly. He's been on the go every minute this summer.

RUTLEDGE [*With a sigh*]. It's the restless age. Poor boy, I know; it's the time when fruit that's good to the eye is ashes to the mouth. "You seize the flower," as they say, "and its bloom is shed."

MRS. RUTLEDGE. I do wish he'd settle down.

RUTLEDGE. My dear, he's only twenty. [*There is a pause.*] Will you send him in when he comes?

MRS. RUTLEDGE. Are you going to wait up?

RUTLEDGE. Yes.

MRS. RUTLEDGE. Then, good night, dear.

RUTLEDGE. Good night.

[*He leads her to the door, opens it, kisses her, and she goes out. He settles down to his work again, but has hardly started before the door opens and* LEE *enters, in a manifest and uncontrollable state of excitement.* RUTLEDGE *puts down his pen and rises hastily.*]

RUTLEDGE [*Sharply*]. What is the matter! Why don't you answer, Lee? What is the matter with you?

[LEE *drops into a chair and covers his face with a gesture of blind horror.* RUTLEDGE *goes quickly to the door, closes and fastens it, and returns to where his son is sitting.*]

RUTLEDGE [*Quietly*]. What is the matter, son? You must tell me.

[LEE *finally raises his head, and slowly gets control over himself.*]

LEE. Suppose—just suppose—mind—

RUTLEDGE. Yes, go on!

LEE. Suppose a nigger, a dirty nigger—put his hand on you—

RUTLEDGE [*Sternly*]. Who has done this to you, Lee? What has happened? Come, now; I must know.

[*The negro* JOHNSON, *disheveled, and with a swollen and discolored eye, enters the room through the window. He is holding Lee's soft grey hat, which was knocked off in the struggle, in his hand. The man stands just inside the room, breathing heavily, and glaring uncertainly about him like a wild animal, brought suddenly into the light.* LEE *leaps to his feet with an exclamation of anger and surprise.* RUTLEDGE *steps in front of him and shields him with his body.*]

RUTLEDGE [*To the negro*]. Who told you to come here at this time of night? What do you want, Johnson.

JOHNSON. Ask yo' boy. He knows.

RUTLEDGE. I'm in the habit of sending darkies to my back door, Johnson, and I make no exception for you.

JOHNSON. That didn't keep yo' boy from comin' right into my front do' tonight, without askin' no one's leave. [RUTLEDGE *turns and looks searchingly at his son.* LEE *turns his head away.*]

JOHNSON. I brought his hat to him. Heah it is! [*He tosses it on the table.*] I found him with my girl tonight an' I want to tell you he's lucky to be standing where he is.

RUTLEDGE [*White faced*]. Get out, Johnson.

JOHNSON. All right, I'm goin', but, white man, I want to tell you there ain't never going to be any dealin's between you and me. I'm through with you. [*The negro goes out.* RUTLEDGE *turns to his son.*]

RUTLEDGE. Is this true? [*There is a pause.*]

LEE. Yes, I'll go away.

RUTLEDGE. Go where?

LEE [*Turning away*]. Oh God, I don't know! Anywhere!

RUTLEDGE [*Quietly and firmly*]. You'll do nothing of the sort,
  Lee. Sit down.
LEE [*Writhing desperately*]. Don't talk about it, please.
RUTLEDGE. I'm not going to talk about it. I want you to promise me never to talk about it. Will you promise?
LEE. Yes.
RUTLEDGE [*With steady persuasiveness*]. No matter what hap-
  pens to either of us,—if we are alone together, if we are
  with other people; no matter what worries, troubles, or
  cares we may have; no matter what grief, pain, joy, suf-
  fering, or happiness we know, I want you to act and to
  live as if this day, out of all the other days in our lives,
  had never happened. Promise!
LEE. I promise.
  [*The shadow of a great African head is projected against the
  wall for a moment.*]
    [*The high piping tune, far off.*]

    Curtain

A bedroom suite in the Altamont Inn. The Inn, which is built of gray uncut stone, and roofed in billowing red tile, is in the English style, and is a most fashionable hostelry. All of its apartments are appropriately named. This one bears the title of "YE SNUG-GERIE," stenciled in old English letters aross the door.

There is a living room and a bedroom, furnished tastefully in black walnut. We see both rooms and the partition between.

It is midnight of the same day. A babble of voices is heard before the rise of the curtain. PRESTON CARR is discovered in the living room of his apartment, engaged in conversation with three guests: —BAILEY, SORRELL and PROFESSOR HUTCHINGS. He has been renewing his campaign pledges, engaging in intimate anecdote, and enumerating the qualifications for leadership.

CARR. . . . My friends, you can't fool the people. They know their man. The common judgment of mankind is infallible. Then, what is it that the people demand first of all in one of their servants?

BAILEY. Personality: snap, ginger, pep! He must be a live wire.

CARR. That's part of it; that's another way of saying he must have imagination. Yes, my friends, imagination's the thing.

BAILEY. Vision!

CARR. Yes. That's the same thing, too. When my opponent came out in favor of evolution in his speech at the University, he made the greatest mistake of his political career. He showed no imagination. I took him up like a flash. "Which shall it be?" I said to my constituents, "which shall it be? God or Monkey?" And when election day came, you know the result; they rallied to my standard. That night the eagles of victory were perched aloft on the banner of Preston Carr, while that of J. Vance Lewis dragged in the dust of ignominious defeat.

BAILEY [*Aside to Sorrell*]. He stirs my blood when he talks like this!

SORRELL [*Aside to Bailey*]. He's at his best.

PROFESSOR H. [*Coughing dryly and nervously*]. Strictly speaking, of course, in regard to evolution, the facts . . . .

CARR. The facts! What do we care for the facts? This is politics,—not a census report. It is my duty to appeal to the imagination. I know the facts as well as you do, my dear Professor. But I choose to touch the imagination—and I sweep the state.

BAILEY [*Quoting*]. "Life and life more abundant for all the people of this great State."

CARR. Exactly. There you have it! that's imagination. "God or Monkey! Which?" There you have it again. That's imagination. The thing sticks; their minds take fire at an idea poetically expressed. Gentlemen, in my opinion, God and good weather are the two greatest campaign issues the Democratic party has ever had. As you know, in my campaign I came out in favor of both. I made the point that our great party had always obeyed and feared the one, and controlled the other. And you know the result:—

BAILEY, SORRELL. You swept the State.

CARR. Exactly.

PROFESSOR H. [*Rather timidly*]. Of course the facts in the case . . . .

CARR [*Scornfully*]. The facts! Why, man alive, I *had* the facts! I *used* 'em. I proved conclusively that the only time the Re-

publican party has ever been in power in this state since
the Civil War, we had a falling off in church attendance
and the coldest winter known to history. If those aren't
facts, what are they?

PROFESSOR H. [*Tapping his finger tips*]. You strive for the illu-
sion of a higher reality, as it were . . . the truth that lies
behind reality. Why Governor, you are a philosopher,—
an Aristotelian!

BAILEY [*To Sorrell*]. You heard that, didn't you?

CARR. Of course now that I am in office I intend to recognize
the facts. My name shall be linked to that of Progress.
We shall go forward together. You know my views on the
roads program, the education appropriations bill, the
fisheries endowment, and other progressive measures.
When I go out of office four years from now I want it to
be said that Preston Carr never betrayed a trust he made
to the masses of the people, that he has carried out in full
his campaign promises to his constituents, and that he
has done more for the cause of progress than any governor this state has ever had.

SORRELL. We know you'll do it too, Governor.

BAILEY. Yours will be a notable administration, Governor.

CARR. My friends, I thank you for these expressions of your
confidence. [*He gets up and makes a quick little bow.*]

PROFESSOR H. [*Looking at his watch*]. Much as I hate to disturb
so pleasant and informative a discussion, I think we had
better disperse now. It is past twelve, and the Governor
has a hard day mapped out tomorrow.

BAILEY. Can it be so late? When the Governor speaks, the
hours become minutes.

[*All rise to depart.*]

CARR [*Becoming confidential*]. I don't like to send you boys
away—ahem—empty handed. I am reminded of what

the governor of North Carolina said to the governor of South Carolina. So, if the Professor here doesn't think it will disagree with his academic dignity—[*All laugh heartily.*] we might take a little nip before you go.

PROFESSOR H. [*With rare good humor*]. Ah, Governor, professors may have changed more than you suspect, since you were a student.

CARR. Then—if you'll wait, just a minute, boys. [*He goes into his bedroom.*]

BAILEY. He's a regular fellow in every way, isn't he?

PROFESSOR H. All great men are simple and unaffected in their ways. It's a sure test of their quality.

SORRELL. What a fine figure of a man the Governor is! He carries himself as straight as a rod.

BAILEY. What shoulders he has! He could carry an ox on them! Think of it!—the destinies of this great state are on that man's shoulders for four years. And he sat here talking to us tonight like any plain citizen.

PROFESSOR H. I am disposed to admire the Governor's head more than any other physical attraction he has. What a way he has of tossing it like an angry bull, when denouncing an opponent, or when exposing some vicious and corrupt practice. What a forehead! And what a splendid mane of hair!

[*During this time* GOVERNOR PRESTON CARR *has been preparing the beverage in his bedroom. We see him enter, glance quickly back to see if he is watched, and open his traveling bag, from which he takes a quart bottle, which bears in high letters the word "Alcohol" surmounted by a skull and crossbones. He washes this label off at the basin, and fills the bottle which is already half full, with water, shaking the mixture well, and stirring it around with a pencil, glancing furtively toward the door, he takes a small flask from his hip pocket, drinks deeply, and returns it. This done, he sets the bottle and several glasses on a tray, and returns to the living room. The men make the customary exclamations of joyful surprise.*]

BAILEY. Am I seeing straight!

SORRELL. Right from the old well, eh, Governor?

[*The Governor eyes him sharply.*]

CARR. I hope you'll like this. A constituent sent it to me, and said it was really good corn whiskey. [PRESTON CARR *gives each of his guests a glass and pours for* BAILEY *first.*] Say when!

BAILEY. When!

SORRELL. When!

PROFESSOR H. When!

BAILEY [*Lifting his glass*]. Well,—here's looking at you, Governor!

SORRELL. Wait! I propose a toast! [*They pause.*]

[*He is silent a moment phrasing his toast, then proceeds.*] "May our governor's reign be as successful as his intentions are honest; may he have faithful followers, industrious assistants, and devoted friends; finally, may he achieve for himself what he has so gloriously promised his constituents; "Life and Life more abundant!" [*The three men touch glasses and drink. The Governor bows his acknowledgment.* BAILEY *and* SORRELL *gulp their drinks down; the Professor coughs and gasps a little.*]

CARR. How is it, boys?

SORRELL [*Doggedly*]. Splendid!

BAILEY [*Weakly*]. The best I ever tasted!

PROFESSOR H. [*Wiping his mouth*]. Yes; a strong but not unpleasant beverage.

BAILEY. Aren't you drinking with us, Governor?

SORRELL [*A trifle bitterly*]. Just one, to be sociable, Governor.

[*He takes the bottle and makes ready to pour.*]

CARR [*Hastily*]. No thank you, I don't think I'd better tonight.

BAILEY. Just one, to make it a party, Governor.

CARR [*Feebly*]. I don't think I'd better, really—another time.—
Business tomorrow—

SORRELL [*Boisterously, rather stimulated*]. Ah, come on, Governor. Say when!

[*He pours recklessly and spills some of the beverage on the blot-
ting paper on the table, which immediately bursts into flame.
BAILEY extinguishes it with his hand.*]

BAILEY. Look out, Hen. You're spilling it, man. That's pre-
cious stuff.

SORRELL. Is that enough, Governor?

CARR [*Rather mournfully*]. Yes, plenty, thank you. Well, here's
to you gentlemen. [*He drains the glass rapidly, giving one or
two shuddering gasps at the end.*]

BAILEY. A little strong, but splendid stuff. Thanks for the entertainment, Governor.

CARR. The debt is mine. You must all come again.

SORRELL. Thank you. Good night, Governor.

PROFESSOR H. Good night and pleasant dreams, Governor.
We'll meet soon again, I hope, at the University.

CARR. Yes, boys, I trust we shall. Good night.

[*They all go out. The Governor closes the door carefully when
they are gone. He replaces the tray and glasses, and puts the
bottle in his traveling bag. Returning to the living room he
takes a small, blue volume from his desk, thumbs the pages until he finds what he is looking for, reads intently, puts the book
down, and repeats:*]

Glamis thou art, and Cawdor; and shalt be
What thou art promised.

[*He ponders deeply on this for a moment, then replaces the book
in the desk. He goes to the mirror of his dresser and considers
himself carefully, in all his aspects,—now sternly frowning,
now playfully smiling; now with hands folded before him; now
behind; now profile; now front view. He even takes a small mir-*

ror and revolves slowly in order to see himself from all angles.
This done, the Governor prepares to go to bed; he goes first to
the door, opens it quickly and peers out. He then closes it, locks
it, and pulls on it hard several times to make sure his work is
secure. He wads up a small piece of paper and rams it into the
keyhole with his penknife. Next he draws up a small rug and
arranges it in such a manner as to hide the crack at the bottom of
the door. He cuts several long strips from newspapers, which he
wets in water, and pastes along the edges of the door. He goes to
the 'phone and says to the hotel clerk below: "This is the Honorable Preston Carr. I am not to be called or disturbed by anyone
until nine o'clock tomorrow morning." He goes to the closet,
explores it thoroughly, then closes the door and locks it. He goes
to the window, looks out, down, and to either side, then pulls
the shade completely down and tacks it at the bottom. He looks
behind the dresser, in each of the drawers, under the rug, and
beneath the bed. He comes back quickly and takes a second look
under the bed.

Then, he begins to disrobe, or, we should say, to dismantle
his various parts. First he removes his toupee, folds it with
tender care, and puts it lovingly under his pillow. Then he takes
out a gleaming set of false teeth, which he washes at the basin,
and puts on his dresser. Then he pulls off his shoes and takes out
carefully three sets of false soles, and a pair of leather arches. He
then pulls off his coat and takes from under the shoulders a thick
pair of shoulder pads; then he removes the shoulder braces
which give him his erect appearance. He pulls off his shirt and
unlaces next his abdomen-supporter; an immediate fleshy land-
slide to his middle regions is visible.

He goes behind a chair,—(Here art must supplant photog-
raphy),—and removes his underwear—three suits in all,—
disclosing a flabby, mottled, and wart-pitted torso, which flows
down to the bulging mountain of his belly. Shivering, and displaying evidences of the utmost trepidation, he takes his pa-

jamas *from the chair, and dons them, after which he tiptoes*
softly to the door and listens intently for a moment. Apparently
satisfied, he returns and is about to turn off the lights, when his
image in the mirror again arrests his attention. He pauses,
looks, and mutters toothlessly and incoherently. Failing to un-
derstand himself, he picks up his teeth from the dresser, claps
them into his mouth, and repeats again:)

Glamis thou art, and Cawdor; and shalt be
What thou art promised.

[*He removes the teeth, puts them on the dresser, takes a fright-*
ened survey of the room, and a fugitive look under the bed,
switches the light off, and leaps beneath the cover, which he
pulls securely up as far as his eyes. There is silence and absolute
stillness for a moment. Then in the dim light, the bedclothes
move, the white wedge of his face comes slowly in view, and as
slowly uplifts itself. Slowly, shudderingly, he climbs from his
bed and goes down on his knees, until his face is tilted in prayer,
and his hands folded in supplication. The prayer is silent.

A bright moonbeam intrudes through the crack in the curtain
and gilds his bald head, in poetic phrase, "an unearthly white."

For the benefit of those who have never seen a governor at his
prayer, it is well to explain that, in engulfing darkness, which
blots out line, form and perspective, and which gives a vast and
empty look to things, he often seems no more than a small,
pudgy, and rather terrified boy.

And here, as the story writers say, let us leave him to his
orisons.]

Curtain

SCENE **8**

It is the next morning, and the scene is again the street in Nigger-town brought closer to view until we see only one side of the vacant lot and the building which contains the dirty looking restaurant and the greasy fried foods, and on the other side, separated only by a flimsy board partition, the dark and smoke-filled poolroom.

At first only two young negro men are present on the street. One is a large black negro called SLEW-FOOT, a stupid, sullen-appearing, and thoroughly vicious member of his race. The other is a small mulatto, a little man with a sharp, furtive face, and with no gift for silence, as his rapid, chattering conversation discloses. There is something decidedly ape-like in his appearance, in his volu-ble, high-pitched chattering, in the momentary glimpses he affords us of gleaming white teeth, and in the unbaffled pertinacity of his attempts to promote conversation with his sullen, monosyllabic neighbor. This negro's name is PICKENS GAFFNEY.

This pair will presently be joined by other negro men, some members of the crowd, some important enough to be named.

There comes, from time to time, from another part of the lot, the sound of hammers and the rattling of a cement mixer, indicating that workers are engaged on construction nearby. There is also visi-ble a small pile of sand, used by the mixers of lime and cement.

Affixed to the brick wall is a large, brilliantly colored poster, an-nouncing the arrival in Altamont, on its fortieth annual tour, of the Al G. Fields' Minstrel Troupe. The central part of the poster con-tains a picture of the assembled company, in its wonted semicircle, with the black-face comedians and dancers in suits of red silk at ei-ther end, and the singers, in eighteenth-century periwigs and silks, *in the center. On either corner of the posters are small pictures of the company's chief comedians:* BERT SWOR, JOHN HEALEY, BILLY BEARD,—*white men, and, as the poster says, "Famous for their inimitable portrayal of negro character."*

PICKENS GAFFNEY. I heahs dat Jones woman's in de lock-up again.

SLEW-FOOT [*In surly tones*]. Whut Jones woman?

PICKENS GAFFNEY. Lawd, boy—you ought to know her; you laid up wid her enough: *Carrie Jones.*

SLEW-FOOT. How do I know who you's talkin' 'bout? Dey's mo'n one Jones woman, dey's a million. Speak so's I heah yo', niggah. [*After this, conversation languishes somewhat, but not for long.*]

PICKENS GAFFNEY. Is you gwine to de dance tonight?

SLEW-FOOT. Whut dance? I don't know nothin' 'bout no dance.

PICKENS GAFFNEY. De dance at de Y.M.I.

SLEW-FOOT. How'd I know which dance you'se talkin' 'bout? [*Again there is a lull.*]

PICKENS GAFFNEY. Is yo' seen dat bright-skinned niggah dat's been goin' roun' wid his papahs?

SLEW-FOOT. What bright-skinned niggah? Dey's million bright-skinned niggahs.

PICKENS GAFFNEY [*Showing some sign of irritation*]. Look heah, big boy, don't you evah *see* nothin' so you undahstan's it?

SLEW-FOOT. You got to talk so's I heah you, niggàh. I ain't no mind-readah!

PICKENS GAFFNEY. I mean dat bright-skinned fellah fum de Nawth. He belongs to one o' dem suhsietys whut's gwine to make us as good as de white men.

SLEW-FOOT. How dey gwine to do dat?

PICKENS GAFFNEY. Dey goin' to fix hit so's we kin ride on de same seats in de street kyars wid de white folks, and sit nex' to dem in de shows, and eat in de same eatin' places wid dem.

SLEW-FOOT. Go on, boy! Yo' kin do dat right now in Bawston.

PICKENS GAFFNEY. Sho'! Ain't dey no Jim Crow up dere?

SLEW-FOOT [*Pausing impressively*]. Boy, dey don't know whut it is!

[SAM TIPTON, *a broad-faced, grinning young negro, makes his appearance, and joins the group.*]

PICKENS GAFFNEY. Heah's ole Sam Tipton! When yo' git out, boy?

SAM. Yestiddy.

SLEW-FOOT [*Surlily*]. You been on de gang, ain't yo'?

SAM [*Rather insolently*]. Mus' is, niggah.

SLEW-FOOT [*Belligerently*]. Who tol' you to call me niggah, niggah?

SAM [*Also in a hostile manner*]. Don' call me no niggah, niggah!

SLEW-FOOT. Who de yo' think yo' is, boy? Don't go gittin' biggity 'roun me!

SAM. Shut up, niggah, or I'll call you whut you is!

SLEW-FOOT. Don' you cuss me, niggah!

PICKENS GAFFNEY [*The mediator*]. I heah yo' ole grandaddy's jes' got paid a pow'ful lot o' money by de white folks fo' his place.

SAM [*Proud in the consciousness of newly acquired wealth*]. Sho'! De ole man's lousy wid money. He don' know whut to do wid it.

PICKENS GAFFNEY [*Laughing loudly*]. I reckon you know! Don't you, boy?

SAM. I reckon I does. I'm goin' to hab me some of dat money.

PICKENS GAFFNEY. I wish I had some money right now. I'd pack up an' take a trip Nawth.

SAM. Uh, *uh*, boy! Dat don' go fo' me!

PICKENS GAFFNEY. Sho; you ought to heah de ole Slew Foot tell 'bout Bawston.

SAM. Whut 'bout Bawston, boy?

PICKENS GAFFNEY. Dat place mus' be niggah heaven. Dey ain't no Jim Crow up dere.

SAM. Whut good dat do?

PICKENS GAFFNEY. Ole Slew Foot say you can sit on de same seats an' eat offen de same tables wid 'em.

SAM. Whut good dat do, boy?

SLEW FOOT. Dey treats you like a ginleman up dere, dat's whut. You'se jes' as good as a white man.

SAM. Yes, yo' is! Don' tell me, niggah. Ef all dat eatin' and sittin' wid dem at de tables made you's good as de white folks, whyn't yo' stay up dere wid 'em?

SLEW FOOT [Sullenly]. Aw, I don' like de damn col' weathah dey has.

SAM [Scornfully]. Eatin' at de tables wid 'em, was you? Yes you was! Big boy, when you got back home, you didn' look like you'd been doin' much eatin' wid anyone. Yo' ribs was stickin' out, an' ef dey hadn't sent you on de gang fo' dat cuttin' scrape, you'd a stahved to death. [Other negro men come up from time to time to join the party. They listen in, and occasionally add a remark of their own.]

A NEGRO MAN. Well, hit'll be movin' day fo' us niggahs soon.

ANOTHER. We got ouah awduhs to git out on de fust.

NEGRO MAN. Dat only give us two weeks.

PICKENS GAFFNEY. Wheah is yo' movin' to?

THIRD NEGRO MAN. I'm goin' to wuk fo' de tann'ry an' git one of dere houses down by de tracks. It's closah fo' me dere, anyway.

SECOND NEGRO MAN. You tan'ry folks is all right. But whut 'bout dese othah niggahs? Dey's shuntin' us 'way ovah to de Hollow on de othah side o' town.

FOURTH NEGRO MAN. Don' know how it's goin' to seem bein' so fah off. Dis seems home to me now. I nevah lived nowhere else.

SLEW FOOT. Well, ef I didn't want to go, I wouldn't go, an' dey wouldn' budge me.

SAM. Dat's strong talk, big boy! I'se seen niggahs like yo' befo'; dey's a whole gang of 'em out dere wher' I come from, makin' little 'uns out'a big uns.

PICKENS GAFFNEY [Showing his teeth]. Dat doctah man didn't take none o' dere sass. He tol' 'em he wan't gwine to sell 'less he wanted to.

SAM. Whut's dat got to do wid dese niggahs heah? He owns de house he's livin' in, don' he?

PICKENS [Unwillingly]. Yeah, I 'spec' he do.

SAM. Well, den, whut you talkin' 'bout?

SECOND NEGRO MAN. He come across, dough. He tol' 'em de othah day he'd sell hit.

ANOTHER. Uh, uh, boy! He ain't gwine to now. I seen him dis mawnin'. He say he change his min'.

[A sensation in the crowd, and startled exclamations of "No," "Go on, Boy," and "Sho."]

PICKENS GAFFNEY [Grinning excitedly]. De ole doc ain't lettin' no one boss him roun'.

NEGRO MAN. He's holdin' out fo' mo' money, dat's whut he's doin'.

AN OLDER MAN. He's a damn fool, den. Dey's awffuhed him twice as much as de place is wuth already.

PICKENS GAFFNEY. Ef I was him I'd hol' out till dey awffuhed him three times as much.

OLDER MAN. Yeah, an' you'd tu'n up missin', too. [Laugh] Dose white men ain't gwine to fool wid him.

PICKENS. Dey got to have dat house, ain't dey?

OLDER MAN. Yeah, but dey ain't goin' to lissen to no hold-up.

SLEW FOOT [Getting on center of the stage]. Dat's de way dey does us, now. We was good enough to go to France an' fight fo' 'em; now we ain't good enough to tromp on.

SAM. Uh, *uh*. Lissen to Gen'l Pushing!

[*The other men laugh and nudge each other.*]

SLEW FOOT [*Belligerently*]. Whut you shovin' in fo', boy?

SAM. *You* went to France and fought fo' 'em, didn' you?

SLEW FOOT. Who says I didn'? I kin show you my ticket. De man give me my cahd an' says: "You is 963,437."

SAM. Big boy, you sho' was considduble. But when'd you do any fightin' in France?

SLEW FOOT. Whut'd *you* do, niggah?

SAM. Me? Who said anything 'bout me? You don' heah me goin' roun' braggin' and blowin' 'bout whut I done, does you? No. I didn' do no mo' den you. We was bofe back dere loadin' de boats an' haulin' de truck aroun';—dat's where we was an' dat's de only fightin' you done, niggah, 'cause I was right dere wid you. You ain't nevah seen none o' dose Gummans, boy; you ain't even seen a pictuah uv 'em.

SLEW FOOT [*Sullenly*]. I reckon I'd a gawn ef dey'd sent fo' me.

SAM. Den I reckon dey'd have to a-carried you, boy, 'case you sho-Gawd would'n have been able to wawk.

[*There is a roar of laughter at this sally, and* SLEW FOOT *rewards his persecutor with most evil looks. At this moment* UNCLE AMOS TODD *comes by. As he nears the crowd, his face sets in a heavy scowl; he mutters ominously to himself, and he grips his cane a little more tightly. The negroes, who are in a gay humour now, seize the opportunity to banter the old man a bit.*]

A NEGRO MAN [*Calling loudly*]. Hello, Uncle Amos.

[AMOS *makes no answer, but moves on.*]

ANOTHER. He ain't speakin' to us sence he got his money.

A THIRD. Dat ain't Uncle Amos. Dat's Mistah Jay Pierpont.

[*There is another roar of laughter at this sally; still* AMOS *moves on. Then the young negro* SAM *begins to whistle softly the high piping tune to which the old man appears to keep step. He recognizes immediately the notes of his grandson's voice, and turns angrily, brandishing his cane.*]

AMOS. You nasty, good-fo' nothin' thing, mixin' up wid dat black trash dere. Dey'll git you on de gang agin, dat's whut dey'll do. Ain't you got no shame, boy? You won't wuk, you won't do nothin' but set aroun' wid dat black truck dere. You is jes' plain no 'count an' shif'less,—dat's whut you is. Why ain't you out findin' a job like you would ef you was any good?

SAM [*Innocently*]. Whut fo'? I don' hab to wuk now. You is rich now.

[*There is another burst of laughter from the negroes.*]

AMOS [*Brandishing his cane*]. You don' git nothin' fum me, boy, not a penny. [*He turns away suddenly, but returns again.*] Somebody aught to take a stick to you;—dat's whut you needs. [*He goes on, followed by the laughter of the crowd.*]

[*A tough-looking young white man, wearing leather leggings, a flat cap, and a Norfolk jacket, stops in the street a few feet away and beckons to Sam. The white man is evidently a public chauffeur.* SAM, *wearing his ever-ready grin, shuffles over good-naturedly to him. The negroes talk among themselves in lowered voices, glancing over at the new arrival from time to time, and grinning. The man and* SAM *talk to each other in low tones.*]

THE MAN. Can you git me a quart fer tonight, Sam?

SAM [*After an appreciable pause, in which he appears to ponder*]. Why I reckon so, boss. Co'se, it ain't gwine to be easy to git.

THE MAN. Ah, tie a can to that, an' don't try to hold me up. I can depend on you, can't I? [*With a wink.*] I'm gittin' this fer a guy that wants it awful bad.

SAM. Yes, suh, boss, I'll be heah; at whut time?

THE MAN. I'll come by at eight o'clock.

SAM. All right, boss, I'll have it fo' you, sho.

THE MAN. So long.

[*He goes out.* SAM *returns to the crowd.*]

FOURTH NEGRO MAN. Uh, *uh*, Sam! You sho' is stahtin' in agin, soon. You mus' like dat rock pile.

SAM [*Grinning*]. Well, dey feeds you out dere, boy, and dat's mo'n I gits in heah sometime.

SLEW FOOT. Dey owes us a livin', dat's what. Dey feed us long's we fight fo' em; den dey kicks us when it's all ovah an' we's down.

SAM. Go on, boy! Why don' you git out an' git you a job an' quit yo' growlin'.

SLEW FOOT. Dey ain't no jobs.

SAM. I'll git you a job ef you wants one. De Tan'ry wants men right now. Why don' you go down dere ef yo' wants to wuk? [SLEW FOOT *makes no reply.*] Go on, boy. I *knows* you. You wouldn' take no job ef dey come beggin' you. You wants to sit 'roun' an' growl.

PICKENS. I got one o' dese papahs heah dat dis bright-skinned niggah fum de Nawth has been passin' 'roun.' [*He produces a newspaper from his pocket.*]

SAM. Boy, you'll come up missin', sho, ef you reads dat truck.

PICKENS. Look at dis heah pictuah, will yo'? [*They all crowd around.*] You see dis heah niggah in unifawn wid a gun in bofe han's. He's cuttin' loose on dose white folks ovah dere, an' it say: "An eye fo' an eye; a toof fo' a toof.'"

SLEW FOOT. Heah! Lemme see dat, boy. [*He takes the paper and studies the picture with signs of evident satisfaction.*] Dat's de way to do 'em!

SAM. You'll wake up an' fin' yo'sef graveyahd dead some mawnin', niggah. You'se gittin' too big to be healthy.

ONE OF THE NEGROES [*Sings*].

"Oh, I tell you de graveyahd's a mean ole place,

Dey puts you in de groun' an' throwd d'ut in yo' face."

SEVERAL [*Joining in the chorus*].

"Oh tell me how long

Will I have to wait,

Can I git you now,

Or must I hes-o-tate?"

SAM. De man in de minst'el show sung dat las' yeah. Does you remembah dat little dance he done wid it?

[*He produces a pair of wooden bones from his pocket, rattles them deftly between his fingers, and dances a shuffling clog dance accompanied by strokes of the hand, and rooster-like cranings of the head. The negroes are delighted.*]

ONE OF MEN. Sho! You ought to be in a minst'el show yo'se'f, Sam. De circus dat was through heah las' yeah had a show all of niggahs.

SAM. Dat wan't no good. I seen hit; hit takes de white folks to put on a good minste'l show.

PICKENS. Field's Minst'els is in town today. [*He points to the poster.*]

SAM. You know who's goin' to be dere, too, don't you? When's de peerade?

PICKENS. Dey comes up on de Squah at twelve o'clock, de papah say.

SAM. Boy, I'll be dere "when dat brass ban' stahts playin.'"

[*A small mulatto negro, very well dressed, and wearing spectacles to which a cord is attached, appears in the street bearing a sheaf of newspapers under his arm. The negroes regard him curiously.*]

PICKENS [*In a whisper to the group*]. Dere's dat bright-skinned niggah fum de Nawth.

SAM. Uh, *uh*! Ain't he somp'n, dough! Look at dat strut!

[*The negro surveys the scene for a moment, espies the minstrel poster on the side of this brick wall, goes up to it, and tears it off. This action manifestly pains* SAM *deeply, for he loves the bright colors.*]

SAM [*Protesting*]. Look out, dere, big boy! Whut yo' doin'?

THE MAN [*Using very good English with a New England accent*]. I'm asking you to stand up for your rights, my friends. We'll put an end to the white man's conspiracy for once and for all. This is all part of their propaganda to make a race of buffoons out of us.

SAM. Sho'! Is dey tryin' to do dat?

[*The negroes gather around their Northern brother, staring at him curiously.*]

THE MAN. A minstrel show, my friends, think of it,—a minstrel show made up of white men who poke fun at our race. It's all part of the capitalistic government which wants to keep us down. I'm surprised that you have stood for it so long. Where I come from we wouldn't tolerate it five minutes.

SAM. Where is you f'um, big boy?

THE MAN [*Coldly*]. My name is Sykes.

SAM [*Unruffled*]. Where is you f'um, Sykes?

THE MAN. I'm from Boston. [*He pauses for this to take effect. They press in close, gazing on him with open-mouthed wonder.*]

SAM. Don't dey have no minst'el shows up dere?

SYKES. Not until a committee of citizens of our race have decided that it contains no matter that would insult or injure our feelings.

SAM. An' whut ef hit does, big boy?

SYKES. Why, we protest to the mayor.

PICKENS [*Triumphantly*]. Uh, uh! Yo' heahs dat, don't you? Dat's de place fo' me. I'se goin' soon's I git de kyar fayah.

SAM. Hush yo' mouf' boy. Don' you want t'see no mo' minst'el shows?

SYKES. Now, my friends, I have a few copies of a newspaper

which should be in the home of every person of color in America:—the Clarion Call. I'm going to give a copy to each of you today and I hope you read it carefully and manage to take out a year's subscription as well. [*He begins to pass copies of the paper around.*]

PICKENS. Dis heah's de same as de one I showed you.

[*A white man, evidently a foreman of laborers or a mason comes by, putting the lid on his dinner pail.*]

SAM. Is yo' through eatin', Mistah Jim?

THE MAN. Yes. You can finish out the can, Sam; there are some sandwiches left. Put the pail back when you get through. [*He goes on.* SAM *puts the dinner pail down by the side of the building.*]

SYKES [*Who has finished distributing the paper*]. Now, my friends, I hope you will all come to hear me when I speak tonight at your local Y.M.I.

SAM. Yo' picked a bad night, big boy. De minst'el show's in town.

SYKES. Surely, my friends, you wouldn't go to a minstrel show, which will only insult and make fun of you, when you can come and hear me explain the purpose of that wonderful organization in the North which is doing so much to promote and alleviate your condition?

PICKENS. Does you belong to dis heah sahsiety I heahs so much about?

SYKES. I am one of its traveling secretaries.

SAM. Whut's de name of dis heah sahsiety?

SYKES. Its full title is the Society for the Promotion of Brotherly Love, Racial Equality, and Humanitarian Principles Between the Colored and White People. If any of you are ever in trouble of any kind, my friends, just write us and we will respond with friendly and sympathetic advice.

PICKENS. Ain't dey no shawt way of sayin' dat name?

SYKES. I'll write it out for you.

SAM. Dat's sho' a considdable sahsiety.

SYKES. My friends, I come to you with tidings of a better day—a day when strife and bitterness will have died from the earth, when hatred, and prejudice will have passed away, when the color line is a thing of the past, and when black men and white men will live together as the brothers they are and should be.

A VOICE. You tell 'em, big boy!

SAM. Whut ef de white men don't want to be brothahs?

SYKES [*Fiercely*]. Then we'll force them;—our dream of brotherhood must be realized and realized it will be, if we have to shoot down the first white man that gets in our way.

SLEW FOOT. Now you's talkin'!

SAM. Yeah, he's talkin', niggah, but he'll be pushin' daisies 'fo' long, ef he keeps dat up!

SYKES. Tonight I am going to talk to you of the infamous plot of the white men of your town who want to rob you of your homes in order to fill their own pockets with the wealth you have created for them.

[SAM *observes at this moment that a crafty black hand has crept over to where the dinner pail sits and has removed the lid. A well-directed kick sends the hand flying away.*]

There is one thing and only one which is needed to raise you from your present condition to your proper place as the equals of the whites. [*He pauses.*] That thing is education.

[SAM *rescues the pail and spits upon the food, covering it with his own saliva, in order to protect it from further depredations. He then puts the pail back with an insolent smile of triumph and is rewarded, by the would-be thief, with a savage look of anger.* SYKES *has busied himself by tacking up a printed bill announcing his lecture, on the space formerly occupied by the minstrel poster. He now prepares to depart.*] Remember, the time is tonight at eight o'clock, my friends. I hope you will all manage to come. There is no admission charge.

[JOHNSON *appears in the street, a grim and unsmiling figure. His manner forbids and repels the negroes, who become suddenly quiet and make a path for him, as he comes by. Finally the curiosity of* PICKENS GAFFNEY *emboldens him to speak.*]

PICKENS. I heah you ain't sellin' de house aftah all, Doctah.

JOHNSON [*Curtly*]. You hear a lot, don't you? [*He turns abruptly and faces the silent, abashed group.*] No. I ain't sellin'! They can't make me get off. I'm not like some folks who let themselves be kicked aroun' from pillar to post.

A MAN. I reckon we got to go when they tells us, Doc. We ain't like you—we don't own nothin', so whut can we do?

JOHNSON [*Contemptuously*]. Yes, you have to go! Of co'se you do; you'll go wherever they tell you whenever they crack the whip. But if you stood up like men you wouldn't have to go anywhere. They couldn't budge you.

SYKES [*Applauding with his hands*]. Hear! Hear!

PICKENS. How do you mean, Doc? De white man owns de place, don't he?

[*There are exclamations in the crowd and a general gathering in. Someone says, "Git up dere and tell us 'bout it, Doc," and others say, "Dat's right, git up dere, Doc." The negro appears to hesitate a moment, but finally he gets up on the little mound of sand which the masons nearby have been using.*]

JOHNSON [*From the mound*]. Yes, the white man owns the place, but you've paid him rents enough to have bought it four times over. Now, when he sees a chance to make more money, he'll kick you off without carin' whether you freeze or starve.

SYKES. It's all part of the capitalist conspiracy to crush our race, just as I . . . . . [*Cries of, "Shut up," "Hush," "Be quiet, man."*]

JOHNSON. If you were white men living down here, do you suppose these people in town would kick you off like this? [*There are cries of "NO!" from the crowd.*] No! The white man knows too much for that. He knows that his own kind are men, and expect to be treated like men, and fight back like men. He thinks that you are dogs and will whine like a dog when he kicks you, and he does with you just as he likes.

A VOICE. Dat's right, Doc. We's as good as de white men. De bright-skin man say so.

JOHNSON. No, niggah, you ain't as good as he is. You're a long way from it. You ain't even as good as I am.

SYKES [*Glibly*]. Education will change all that.

JOHNSON. No, it won't; it's mo' than that. You can't give a man a few books, you can't teach him to read or write, an' make him ovah. I've known white men that couldn't read, but they held their heads up and lived in their own homes, and took care of their women-folks and fought for 'em. The white man makes laws for himself and makes you live up to 'em. He builds jails an' puts you in 'em. His wife bears children an' your wife nurses 'em. The white man believes in a thing an' sticks to it an' fights for it. What do you do? All of you have worked for the white man; you have run his errands an' done his chores all yo' life. An' what's he done fo' you? I'll tell you what he's done. He's given you all them yellow skins I see down there. He's crep' up behind yo' houses in the dark an' gone to bed with your wife an' daughter; an' if she spoke to him in the street the next day he'd knock her down with his fist. That's the white man fo' you! [*He laughs with light-throated madness—his yellow eyes dilating. Angry cries in the crowd.*] If you serve the white man, he'll pay you. If you bow and scrape to him, he will have a good word for you. If you act like a monkey befo' him, he will laugh at you an' give you money. But act like a man and he'll hate you, and he'll want to kill you. [*Excited murmurs and shouts, and a general pressing in.*]

VOICE IN CROWD. Whut we goin' to do, Doc?

JOHNSON. What yo' goin' to do? Why, yo'll do like you always done, niggahs. Yo'll take it lyin' down. [*With sudden fierce exhortation.*] Why don't yo' do like I do? Stand on yo' feet an' act like a man, an' take yo' chances. When they come to put you off the place, tell 'em you ain't goin' to move, an' they can't do anything to you. How can they? Tell 'em you've paid their rents, an' if they give you time you'll buy their houses, but that this is your town an' they can't take it from you an' kick you out to build up anothah. [*There is a roar of approval from the men, and shouts of "You tell 'em, Doc," "That's the way to do it," and so on.*]

VOICE IN CROWD. Who's gwine to stay wid us, Doc, an' tell us whut to do?

JOHNSON. Me. I'll stick to you as long as you stick to me. [*Another roar from the crowd.*]

SLEW FOOT. We's wid you, Doc! We'll stick to you, doc!

SAM [*Pleasantly scornful*]. Don' lissen to de black bastahds, Doc. Dey can't stick to nothin'. [*Cries of anger and disapproval in the crowd.*]

SLEW FOOT [*Menacingly*]. Who's you callin' a black bastahd, niggah?

SAM. I'se callin' you all, but I'se lookin' at you, big boy.

SLEW FOOT. Wait till I git my knife, niggah! [*He reaches for it.*]

JOHNSON. Come on, niggahs! None o' that, now. If you stick to me, I'll . . . .

[SLEW FOOT *and* SAM *engage in a fist fight, and roll over on the ground, clawing, punching, kicking, and cursing, both making hasty but fruitless attempts to draw their knives. In a moment all is turmoil and confusion. The negroes divert their attention from* JOHNSON *and follow the squirming contestants slowly down the lot, shouting advice and encouragement to them as they roll and jostle each other along. Presently the crowd has moved to a point some distance away, leaving* JOHNSON *alone on his pile of sand. He has been trying to attract their attention by shouts, by gestures of the arm, and in various other ways, but they pay no attention to him.*

The man SYKES, *who has been left behind, presently goes over and joins the crowd. And now, above the confusion, there is the sound of music, of a blaring, brass band, and of the beatings of big drums. At first it is barely audible, then it comes closer and closer until it predominates above the shouts and curses of the men.*

A flurry in the crowd is noticeable; the negroes look at each other and cry joyfully, "Minst'el Show! Minst'el Show!" The two fighting men are pulled apart and placed on their feet, and in a moment the whole, howling, jostling pack, SYKES *included, rush out and up the street to the direction of the music, leaving* JOHNSON *standing alone and staring glassily before him.*

Presently he comes down from the sand pile and, as if unconscious of his act, bends and scrapes up a handful of the sand.

The poster that Sykes has nailed to the wall attracts his attention, his big fist tightens convulsively, and the sand spurts out through his fingers. He reads the poster and with a savage gesture tears it from the wall, crumpling it and throwing it to the ground behind the poster of the minstrel show.

The heavy blaring music, and the heavy booming drums, now swoop down upon the stage in great rhythmic beats of sound. It seems as if it is advancing steadily to this point; it seems as if, in a great crash of noise, it will presently converge, on the scene before us. The music is the same foolish recurrent tune that has been previously whistled.

The negro turns, with stolid and unyielding features, and walks rapidly away down the street, in a direction opposite to that taken by the crowd.]

Curtain

The offices of the Altamont Development Company one week later.
It is late afternoon of a gray foggy day, and the stenographer,
MISS NEELY, *wearing coat and hat, is closing and locking her desk,*
preparatory to departure for home.

MISS NEELY *goes to the window nervously and peers out. Ev-*
erything is unnaturally still outside, but, from time to time, there
comes a low hum of voices. SORRELL, *rather haggard and drawn*
about the face, enters the office. He speaks quietly, but it is evident
that he is in a subdued state of excitement.

SORRELL. Leaving, Helen?

MISS NEELY. Yes, sir . . . . [*She continues to peer out.*]

SORRELL. Nervous?

MISS NEELY. I wish those men would go away. The way they
    stand around in little groups and talk, and are quiet
    when you pass by, is enough to make your flesh crawl.

SORRELL. Go home and get a good night's rest. You're tired
    and nervous after these last few days. When you come in
    tomorrow morning everything will be settled.

MISS NEELY. Oh, Mr. Sorrell, I *do* hope—

SORRELL [*Soothingly*]. Nothing's going to happen. We'll work
    the whole thing out around the table before another
    hour.

MISS NEELY. I'm so glad. You don't know what a relief it will
    be.

SORRELL. Yes; it will be for us all.

MISS NEELY. Good night, Mr. Sorrell.

SORRELL. Good night, Helen. [*She goes out.*]

[*Presently there is a babble of voices in the hall, and* SORRELL *looks at his watch.* PROF. HUTCHINGS, *the* REV. MR. SMALL-WOOD, *the Baptist minister, the* HONORABLE MR. SINCLAIR, *the mayor, and* MR. TYSON, *the President of the Centre-Union Bank and Trust Co., come in.*

THE REV. MR. SMALLWOOD, *who is the idol of his flock, is a big, red-faced, well-fed man, in the mid-forties, and wears a white vest. He is hearty in speech and manner; his robust pronunciation of the word 'Brother' warms the cockles of the heart.*

SINCLAIR, *the mayor, like Preston Carr, is a man of the people, and they know it and made him mayor for it. He is a small, provincial, Southerner with all the flamboyance, all the floridity of the clan: to this he combines a hard, peasant hostility toward any idea he cannot understand, so that he holds half the world in constant suspicion.*

TYSON *is small, brisk and plump, in a pasty, white manner; he has all the hard, self-congratulatory assurance of the very common man who has "got there,"—who won his spurs and proved his honesty and worth by fifteen years of steadiness, punctuality, and abstention from tobacco, alcohol, and anything attractive in silk hosiery.*]

SINCLAIR [*As he enters, in angry, querulous tones*]. Johnson hasn't done all of this. It's that educated nigger from the North who's been stirring them up with his speeches and papers. [*More composedly.*] But a flare up, gentlemen, only a flare up. The good people of both races . . . .

TYSON. The man should be driven out of town. He's a menace to law and order.

[BAILEY *rushes in, in a very excited state, brandishing a newspaper in his hand.*]

BAILEY. It's all up! They've let the cat out of the bag. The *New York Times* has a story of the thing on the front page;—all about the troops being sent here and everything.

SINCLAIR [*Angrily*]. Who let the thing out?

TYSON. Oh, the newspapers get hold of everything.

BAILEY [*Fervently*]. Thank God the tourist season's over; it would've knocked an awful hole in our business. I only hope it doesn't hurt us next year.

SMALLWOOD [*Who despises friction*]. I'm sure it'll all be blown over by that time.

BAILEY. It's that Yankee nigger who's behind all this,—mark my words! [*In an aggrieved tone.*] He's quoting books and papers to 'em,—psychology and all,—some of it by niggers, too, saying there's no difference between darkies and white people.

SINCLAIR. I'll bet you anything the black scoundrel is in Republican employ. I see the whole thing. They plan to undermine the foundations of white supremacy in the South again, reestablish black legislatures and free lunch counters in every state capitol, and turn the country over to martial law, corrupt politics, and Northern carpetbaggers. The whole trick is as plain as the nose is on your face.

SMALLWOOD [Butter-lipped]. It is plain, we must do something to refute these infamous assertions.

SINCLAIR. We must do something—but what? [*Helplessly.*] The man is quoting books. It isn't fair! Calling science to his aid, like that.

PROFESSOR H. We can meet his facts with facts of our own, Mr. Mayor. He has only been able so far to quote as authorities three books by sociologists, four by psychologists, and six by economists and historians, a total of thirteen in all, including a total mass of evidence of six thousand, seven hundred, and forty-two pages. Off hand I am able to produce the works of five sociologists, six psychologists, and eight economists and historians, a total of nineteen, composing in all over ninety-five hundred pages of solidly documented scientific, historic, and economic evidence, all tending to show that the negro is racially, morally, intellectually, and physically an inferior. One, indeed, asserts he is a higher species of ape and produces eight hundred closely filled pages to support his contention.

SINCLAIR. Truth will prevail! You have done an invaluable service for science, Professor.

PROFESSOR H. You are doubtless familiar with the famous Bunsen burner experiment of Stiggins?

SINCLAIR. I have forgotten the details for the moment. Will you refresh my memory?

PROFESSOR H. A Bunsen burner is ignited and adjusted to a steady white flame which burns at constant heat. A white guinea pig is then brought forward and the Bunsen burner is placed in close proximity to the animal's left rump. [*The Baptist minister coughs.*] A purely scientific use of the word, sir.

SMALLWOOD [*Relieved*]. Oh, I beg your pardon, Professor.

PROFESSOR H. Not at all. The leap of the white guinea pig in response to the heat stimulus, is now measured. Then the black guinea pig is brought forward, the Bunsen burner is placed in juxtaposition to his—hem—posterior, and his leap measured. Now here is the interesting and decisive thing, gentlemen: during the course of thousands of these experiments, ranging over a period of eight years, Professor Stiggins found that the response of the white guinea pig resulted in an average leap of fourteen and three-quarters inches,—that of the black species in only twelve and one-eighth inches.

BAILEY. Barely a foot.

PROFESSOR H. Exactly! You will find the whole story of this famous experiment set forth in Professor Stiggins' doctoral thesis, published by the University.

SINCLAIR [*Writing in a small book*]. I must get that down. What is the title?

PROFESSOR H. The Locomotive Response of Black and White Guinea Pigs to Heat Sensation.

BAILEY [*In open-mouthed wonder*]. Well, what do you know about that!

TYSON [*Looking at his watch*]. See here. When are they going to start this thing off?

SORRELL. We're ready to start, gentlemen, as soon as Mr. Rutledge and Colonel Grimes arrive.

[*At this moment, the rest of the party comes in. It includes* WEBSTER, *the publisher of the morning paper, a small, weazened, sourfaced man;* KENDALL, *his editor, a professional newspaper man—tall, thin, rather dissipated and sleepy-looking, and wearing eyeglasses;* MRS. WHEELER, *as the representative of the Federated Women's Clubs; and* MR. RUTLEDGE, *who enters from the inner office and seats himself at the foot of the table.*]

TYSON [*Surlily*]. A mistake calling the local guard out. Shouldn't have been sent!

SINCLAIR [*Genially*]. Pshaw, man! A flare up! No more than that.

[COL. GRIMES *comes in unattended. He is a man of some fifty years, with grizzled grey hair, blunt forceful features, with a sphinx-like fixity of expression, and an erect, sturdy figure.* SORRELL *beckons him to a seat at the head of the table. He seats himself. Everyone is trying to talk at once, there is a confused, excited, and angry babble of voices. The army man waits impatiently for the noise to die down, his manner indicating a certain contempt for the lack of order and discipline.*]

GRIMES [*In a harsh, even curiously inflexible voice*]. You sent for me. I am here. What do you want?

SORRELL [*Very smoothly*]. Yes, Colonel. We want the benefit of your advice and suggestion. [*Pause.*] Now I suppose you all know the purpose of this meeting. We are all here to talk over this—this—little disturbance and to discuss ways and means of settling the matter.

BAILEY. It's a splendid idea! Nothing's really the matter. I've said that all along. A good get-together will iron the whole thing out.

SORRELL. I feel there is no essential difference between us and the—ah—colored citizens of this community. The whole matter may be settled by the use of a little tact.

SMALLWOOD [*Beaming*]. Ah yes, tact, Brother Sorrell. Tact. And faith! Oh, my friends, we must have faith,—faith in ourselves, faith in mankind, and, above all, faith in the blood of the lamb. [*A noise in the street*]. Won't some-one close the window? I think we can talk better then. [BAILEY *gets up and shuts the window.*] The church must rise to its new duties, Brethren. We must take life as it comes to us. We must reclaim our poor, strayed sheep, we must—

SORRELL [*Leading him off*]. Yes. Exactly! Now, Colonel Grimes, we'd like to get your opinion. What do you think?

GRIMES [*In his harsh, even, subdued voice*]. Think! Why, sir, I think it's all a very good idea. [*They pause, waiting to hear more. He closes his gray mouth firmly, and looks at them with stony eyes.*]

SORRELL. Now, if anyone has any helpful suggestions—any little thing that you think might help!

MRS. WHEELER. I'd like to say that the Associated Women's Clubs are ready to do all they can to help at any time. We will be glad to make sandwiches and coffee—that is, if anyone needs them. [*There is a pause while everyone consid-ers this. Then—.*]

SORRELL. All right. Has anyone else any suggestions?

TYSON [*Exploding with a suddenness which makes them jump*]. I didn't come here to talk faith, hope and charity! My good money's tied up in this thing. I want some protection. My property is endangered. I'd like to ask the Colonel what he intends to do.

GRIMES [*In the same inflexible tone*]. I will wait.

WEBSTER. Wait!

[*Several, in particular* TYSON, *the banker,* SINCLAIR, *the mayor, and* WEBSTER, *the publisher, speak at once. Again there is the tumult, but from the confusion our ears pick out these phrases:*]

>   . . . rights of property
>   . . . must have protection
>   . . . sin and shame
>   . . . disgrace to the community
>   . . . no respect for law
>   . . . laughing-stock of State

[*And so on.* THE COLONEL, *as before, waits inflexibly until the hubbub dies down.*]

WEBSTER. What of the burning of those two shacks?

GRIMES. White men—perhaps.

WEBSTER [*Excitedly*]. Can you prove that? Can you?

GRIMES. Ask the editor of your paper.

[*They turn to* KENDALL, *the editor. He wets his lips nervously and turns questioningly to his employer,* WEBSTER.]

KENDALL [*Quickly*]. An unidentified mob!

TYSON [*Bluntly*]. Who?

GRIMES [*With a frozen smile*]. Ah!

SMALLWOOD [*Deprecatingly—rubbing his hands*]. I am sure only the riff-raff and scum of creation take part in these affairs. The better class of citizens—

SORRELL. Now, is there anyone else? Mr. Rutledge, have you any suggestion?

[MR. RUTLEDGE *raises his head slowly and with effort, and we see now that his face is old and gray.*]

RUTLEDGE [*Quietly*]. Colonel Grimes, I thought I wanted a house. I am no longer sure.

WEBSTER [*Hotly*]. What are you talking about, Rutledge? You're not the only one interested in this business.

SORRELL [*Tactfully*]. Of course, Mr. Rutledge, none of us want violence.

SMALLWOOD. Oh, no indeed.

BAILEY. By no means.

SORRELL. It's merely the principle of the thing we're standing up for.

RUTLEDGE. The principle of the thing?

SORRELL. Well,—the principle of law and order.

RUTLEDGE. My friend, that is nonsense. We don't fight for principles.

WEBSTER [*Angrily*]. This is a fine time you've taken to turn against us! But my money and other people's money is in this business as well as yours. And we're not going to see our property destroyed without an effort.

RUTLEDGE [*With a passionate cry*]. What does it matter, if we can't have it fairly!

[*They start to their feet and face one another. There is again confusion around the table.*]

SORRELL [*Pacifically*]. Gentlemen, gentlemen!

SMALLWOOD [*Hastily pulling out his watch and consulting it*]. Oh dear me! I really must be going. I'm already late for an engagement at the parsonage. [*He rises. So, too, do* PROF. HUTCHINGS *and* MRS. WHEELER.]

PROFESSOR H. Then I'll accompany you, sir. Everything is getting along so nicely—[*Waves his hand.*] Anyway, I just dropped in for a few minutes.

MRS. WHEELER. Now, remember, we are always ready to help with sandwiches and coffee.

[SMALLWOOD *moves out of the room, murmuring, "Faith,*

*faith, my brothers . . . Yes,—and tact." He goes out, followed
by* PROF. HUTCHINGS *and* MRS. WHEELER, *he gallantly giving
the lady precedence.*]

    [*They go out and the door is closed behind them.* TYSON, *who
has also gotten to his feet, now speaks across the table to Rutledge, and his voice betrays a cold, unreasoning antagonism.*]

TYSON. Rutledge, what I've got, I've got by main strength,
    not by sentiment. I've pulled myself up by my own boot-
    straps. No one ever pampered me. Your father was a rich
    slaveholder. Mine was a poor farmer. All right. That was
    well and good fifty years ago. But, by God! we've come
    far since then, and you haven't kept up with us. And we
    intend to hold on to what we have.

WEBSTER. Stop living in the past, Rutledge. That day is gone.

RUTLEDGE [*Slowly and quietly*]. No. A day I have never seen.
    Money changers, I am no part of your scheme. I wanted
    a house—I wanted a house, but now I want nothing!

    [*Again there is the confusion of voices, during which the door
opens and a* GUARDSMAN *comes in. He goes directly to Colonel
Grimes, saluting, and whispers to him.* THE COLONEL *speaks
to him but we do not hear what he says. A hush falls over the
group, and they turn questioningly to the officer.*]

GRIMES. I declare this town under martial law. I request all
    you people to go at once to your homes and wait there
    until you receive further instructions.

    [*He goes out immediately. There is stunned silence for a mo-
ment; then the quiet is broken by the heavy reverberations of the
fire bell beating out the number of the alarm. A moment later
the trucks thunder by outside, with a rapid clanging of bells.*
SORRELL *leaps to his feet and rushes to the window, looking
away toward the settlement.*]

SORRELL. By God! They've fired the place.

    [*All the men, except Rutledge, rush to the window, and there is again a great deal of noise, mingled with oaths and curses.* RUTLEDGE *sits at the table as if unmindful, with his back toward the window.*]

WEBSTER [*Savagely*]. Niggers this time! There's no doubt of it. [*They become quiet again, and then turn and gaze questioningly at one another and at the bent figure of Mr. Rutledge at the table. Then all except Sorrell file slowly and softly out. A red glare lights the windows.* MR. RUTLEDGE *sits stolidly at the table.*]

SORRELL [*After a moment*]. Mr. Rutledge!

RUTLEDGE [*Very quietly, almost inaudibly*]. My house, Sorrell!

SORRELL [*After a pause*]. Yes. . . . I'm sorry!

[*Then he falls to cursing softly and monotonously, under his breath, while he rummages in one of the drawers of his desk. His mouth is drawn in tight and savage lines. Presently he finds what he is looking for—an automatic revolver. He drops it into the pocket of his coat, jams on his hat, and prepares to quit the room. He again stops to notice the man at the table, and again he speaks to him very quietly.*] Are you coming, too?

[MR. RUTLEDGE *makes no answer, but sits staring before him as if carved from stone. Presently* SORRELL *goes out quietly and closes the door behind him.*]

[*It has begun to grow dark. The glow of the burning house brightens the scene, and its glare paints the windows the red color of blood.* MR. RUTLEDGE *doesn't move in his chair.*]

Curtain

The scene is in the basement of a brick building and represents the interior of the shoe repair shop, conducted by the aged negro, AMOS TODD. *At the rear a narrow flight of steps descends from the sidewalk; a little to the left there is a window which looks out on the level of the pavement and which admits through its dirty panes a dim, unsatisfactory light.*

The machinery of the room is of the simplest and most primitive kind; there is to the right a stitching machine; in the center of the place is a long bench which supports trays of nails, tacks, and repair tools, as well as pieces of leather, and so on.

AMOS TODD *sits by his bench on a chair which has lost its back and whose legs have been sawed off to a convenient shortness.*

For comfort he has provided himself with a worn leather cushion such as are used in automobile roadsters.

The old man is engaged in putting half soles on a pair of shoes. Presently he puts aside his hammer and, gripping the shoe between his knees, cuts off the projecting edges of leather with a short knife.

Shoes, ready for delivery, patched in a rude but serviceable fashion, are piled on the bench, and on shelves along the left wall.

Once the old man leaves his stool and goes to the window where he stands quietly a moment and listens.

The street outside is bare of traffic; there are no pedestrians and very little sound, though from a distance may be heard the low hum of many voices. Presently the negro returns to his stool and resumes his work, muttering to himself and shaking his head.

Suddenly, shattering the unnatural stillness, the fire bell begins to ring an alarm; the old man gets to his feet and goes to the entrance; the street outside begins to swarm with activity; feet pass

the window, running; there are cries, exultant, angry or excited.
Afar off rises the sound of the approach of many men; a crescent
hum like the sound of angry bees.

The entrance is darkened by a shadow, and the young negro,
SAM TIPTON, *bounds down into the room.*

SAM. Close up yo' shop an' git along home.

AMOS. Whaffo', Boy?

SAM. De niggahs fired de hill. De white folks is comin' dis
way.

AMOS [*Stubbornly*]. I ain't gwine to budge. De white folks
ain't got no grudge agin me.

SAM. Dey's gwine to be trouble an' dey ain't no use you gittin' mixed up in it. Go on home now, lak I tells you.

AMOS. Lak you tells me! Boy, who is you to tell me? I was in
dis shop befo' you was bawn, boy, an' I been in it, day in,
day out evah since.

SAM [*Impatiently*]. Go on home, now.

AMOS. I goes when it's closin' time, boy. I goes at half past
five lak I allus is done.

SAM [*Looking at the old man's clock*]. Den you only got ten minutes. Go on home.

AMOS. Den I goes in ten minutes, lak I allus has gone. [*A
pause.*] What's you gwine to do, boy?

SAM. Ne' min' 'bout me. I reckon I kin look out fo' myse'f.

AMOS [*Pulling his arm*]. Heah! You stay right wheah you is,
boy. I ain't goin' to lit you git mixed up wid dem no
'count niggahs.

SAM [*Wrenching free*]. Le' go of me. I knows whut I'm doin'.

AMOS. Don' you go fightin' dem white men. You ain't goin'
to git de best of 'em.

SAM. Aw, you ole niggahs ain't got no guts. We's as good as
dey is in a fight. [*He turns to go.*]

AMOS. Don' you go out dere, boy. Ef you does, don' you
evah come back to me fo' nothin'. I'se thoo wid yo'.

[*There are great cries from the other end of the street where the mobs have assembled.*]

SAM. You stay heah an' lay low. You cain't go home now.

AMOS [*Tugging at his arm*]. Come back heah, boy. You stay wheah you is.

SAM. Aw, le' go o' me. I got to see de show, ain't I? [*He wrenches free from the old man's grasp and runs out into the street.*]

   [*There is the sound of breaking glass, and of stones skipping along the pavement, and a stray shot or two. Then with an angry roar, the mobs meet in the street outside. There are oaths, wild screams of rage or pain, the thud of fist on flesh, and all the mingled noises of physical combat. A stone shatters one pane of Amos Todd's window. He goes to the window and looks with a drugged fascination on the scene outside.*

   Suddenly, above the noise, there is the rapid beat of the guardsmen approaching at a double-quick march.

   One hears the hard staccato of military commands, the snapping back of rifle bolts, and a volley of shot, fired over the heads of the combatants.

   There are savage shouts and cries, and the running of many feet along the pavements, as the crowds disperse. The negro JOHNSON, *disheveled, exhausted, and breathing heavily, his mad eyes staring down the steps, runs into the room. He is armed with a revolver.*]

AMOS. Git out of heah! Git out of heah, niggah. I ain't got no place heah fo' de like of you.

JOHNSON. Come away from that window, you old fool.

   [*He attempts to pull him away, but the old man fights him off. There is another volley of gunfire which shatters sill and glass, and the old man is shot down.* JOHNSON *catches him as he falls and drags him to the back of his room and puts him on the floor.*]

   [*Bending over the body.*] I tol' you to come away from there. How bad are you hurt?

   [*There is no answer.* JOHNSON *examines the body briefly.*

The old man is dead. The negro rises slowly and looks down at the inert figure which, with the dirty leather apron, and soiled clothes, looks like a greasy bundle of rags and patches.] You pore ole fool! Whut good's all your bowin' and scrapin' done you?

[*Outside the noise, the shouting, and the confusion have died away in the distance. The guardsmen come by, ordering frightened negroes out of their hiding places, deploying slowly in files on either side of the street. A* GUARDSMAN *discovers the negro* JOHNSON.]

THE GUARDSMAN [*From the top of the steps*]. All right, you! Come out of there! We've got you!

[*The negro turns quickly with a startled cry and leveling his revolver, charges like a bull straight across the room. He is shot down by the* GUARDSMAN, *and pitches forward on his face.*

The GUARDSMAN *comes down into the room, descending the steps very slowly and carefully, and peering cautiously about the room before he enters. He is very young, certainly not twenty, and very frightened.*

A thin somewhat peaked youth, dressed in a uniform some sizes too large for him, and pressing his weapon close to his body, in order to disguise his trembling, he presents anything but a soldierly appearance.

He approaches, with a kind of awed fascination, the figure of the negro JOHNSON, *which stirs slightly. He walks around the figure several times, muttering, "couldn't help it," "couldn't help it," in the manner of a motorist who has run over a dog. Presently he stoops, and very gingerly rolls the body over, face upwards, leaping back and gripping his rifle securely at once.*

A SERGEANT, *a tough, hard-featured young man, enters the room. The* GUARDSMAN *tries to assume a manner of easy matter-of-factness and fails dismally.*]

GUARDSMAN. Right through the lungs, Sergeant.

[*The* SERGENT *bends and examines the body briefly.*]

SERGEANT [*Making a face*]. God! He's bleedin' like a stuck pig!

Here, lend a hand, kid. Go easy; he's still got life in him.
[*They lift the body carefully and carry it to a corner of the room.*]
[COLONEL GRIMES *enters the room.*]

SERGEANT [*In low tone*]. The man's dying, sir.

GRIMES. Send for an ambulance and a doctor.

SERGEANT. Yes, sir.

[*He goes out with the* GUARDSMAN. SORRELL *comes quickly into the room.*]

SORRELL. The house is gone; it burned like tinder.

[*The body on the floor stirs feebly, and the negro speaks in faint tones.*]

JOHNSON. What's that?

[GRIMES *motions* SORRELL *to silence.* RUTLEDGE *enters the room.*]

SORRELL. I'm sorry, sir. The house—

RUTLEDGE [*Briefly*]. Yes, I know. [*He goes to where the body of Amos Todd is lying, and pulls the leather apron away from the old man's face. Then he pulls himself erect with visible effort and stands looking down for a moment.*] That good old man! But why—why?

GRIMES. Oh! Mr. Rutledge, that is the great pity of these matters.

RUTLEDGE [*As if he has not heard*]. Is this, then, the end of loyalty?

[*The dying negro in the corner stirs slightly.* RUTLEDGE *goes to where he is and stands silently a moment, meeting him glance for glance.*]

SORRELL [*In grim, set tones*]. "Those who live by the sword shall perish by the sword."

[*The negro hears, and laughs feebly but mockingly.*]

JOHNSON. He's talkin' to you, I reckon, Colonel.

[SORRELL *has been staring with a fixed, an awful fascination at something which crawls along the warped flooring. Now he plucks nervously at the coat-sleeve of Mr. Rutledge.*]

SORRELL [*In a queer, desperate voice*]. Mr. Rutledge! Come

away! You're getting your feet in it. [MR. RUTLEDGE *does not move.*]

[*A* YOUNG MAN, *brisk, breathless, derby-hatted, runs down the steps into the room.*]

YOUNG MAN. Have you any statement for the papers, Colonel Grimes?

GRIMES [*With a touch of weary irony in his voice*]. Yes, you may say the usual thing: "We have the situation well in hand and expect no further trouble."

YOUNG MAN. Thank you, Colonel. [*He starts to depart, but glances toward the corner.*] Say—what's this?

GRIMES [*Gruffly*]. Something which doesn't concern you—yet. On your way, son.

[*The* YOUNG MAN *goes out unwillingly.*]

RUTLEDGE. Will you leave me alone with this man for a moment?

[*The* COLONEL *inclines his head silently and turns to go.*]

SORRELL [*Moistening dry lips, in a whisper, still gazing at the floor*]. Mr. Rutledge!

[RUTLEDGE *dismisses him with a gesture of the hand.* SORRELL *goes out with* COLONEL GRIMES. *There is a pause when nothing is heard but the faint and labored breathing of the negro. Finally:*]

RUTLEDGE. How are you now?

JOHNSON [*grinning feebly*]. I'm a mad dog, Mistah Rutledge. If you come close I'll bite yo'.

[*There is again a moment's silence.*]

RUTLEDGE. I think we never knew each other, Johnson.

JOHNSON. No, suh. There was somethin' we never quite got over.

[*There is a pause.*]

RUTLEDGE. I am sixty years old, Johnson. Soon I will be an old man [*in a fretful, troubled voice*] and I don't understand. [*A pause.*] My father owned slaves. *Owned* them, body and soul. They've almost forgotten that today, but I remember, [*muttering*] I remember. And now it's as if a dog who had come running to my call should turn and reply in the language of a man. [*A pause.*] I belong to a day that is past.

JOHNSON [*In a puzzled querulous tone*]. An' wheah do I belong?

RUTLEDGE. God knows!

JOHNSON [*He laughs softly and mirthlessly*]. It's even on both sides, I reckon.

RUTLEDGE [*In a voice which is drenched with weariness and despair*]. My life is creeping home on broken feet. All of which I thought myself a part drifts by like painted smoke. Oh, what man is not in bondage to his youth? What man who doesn't see the world go by him at the end? Gone, gone.

JOHNSON. The house?

RUTLEDGE. Gone,—but it doesn't seem to matter!

JOHNSON [*Laughing softly and feebly, but with a note of wonder in his voice*]. No. . . It's funny! . . . All my life I've been fightin' somethin', outside o' me,—then you see it ain't outside at all . . . It's funny . . . Fool niggahs! buyin' oil to make their hair straight! . . . [*He laughs convulsively.*] . . . Like that'd help . . . It's mo'n that . . . It's somethin' heah . . . you see [*taps his chest.*] It's got to come from there. [*With a note of anger.*] They quit on me . . I might've known . . . it didn't do no good . . . [*with a note of triumph in his voice.*] But if I'd been alone . . . I'd rather I had been. [*There is a pause.*]

JOHNSON [*Very faintly*]. It's funny. It's funny . . . [*He is seized by an awful, an uncontrollable fit of laughter, and his whole frame is shaken, though the sound is very feeble, almost inaudible. He tries to speak two or three times, but sputters, and is set off again in the terrible almost silent chuckling.*]

RUTLEDGE. Poor fool! Why did you choose to become a man?

[*In the street there are again signs of activity—again there is traffic, the sounds of noises, voices, even of laughter; again the whistles blow, the siren shrieks its blast, the court house bell booms out its solid six strokes.*

And again—but this time by the window—the workmen come by, marching solidly and heavily in their mortar stiffened shoes, moving as one, feeling as one, compact, a unity, in their implacable animal strength. And so, they pass and are gone.

It grows darker. The lamps in the street go on. There is a fog in Altamont, and it drifts across the street, before the windows, like crimson smoke. Occasionally, there are soft padding footfalls along the pavements, and presently, out of the mist, black faces appear, which press and flatten their broad features against the dirty window panes, peering cautiously and stupidly down on the scene within. Faint and far is heard the high, piping notes of the foolish, futile little tune which was played in the beginning. It grows louder and louder, and deeper and deeper, becoming slow and more slow, until suddenly it ends close at hand in ponderous bass and gutteral notes. MR. RUTLEDGE *continues to stare down with the same grave intentness.*

Curtain

APPENDIX
Two Contemporary Critiques

The audience for the performances of the 47 Workshop plays came by invitation only, and although the mailing list was long, it was considered a privilege by the Cambridge and Boston theatergoers to be included. For each production, there were usually two performances at Agassiz House Theater, which seated over 250 people. The guests were asked to send their comments on the play to Professor Baker, who after reading them passed them along, with the signatures removed, to the author. As a consequence, the young playwrights received a very large number of written responses, many of them very helpful for their future work.

Only two of the comments on Welcome to Our City *have survived. Both are in the Wolfe papers at the University of North Carolina Library and are reprinted here with the permission of Mr. H. G. Jones, librarian of the North Carolina Collection. Critique Number One is especially perceptive: if Wolfe had followed the suggestions for cuts, particularly of the self-pitying remarks of Rutledge in the closing scene, his play would have received a Broadway production.*

CRITIQUE NUMBER ONE:

Mr. Wolfe's play is to me quite the most interesting piece of work that I have seen at the Workshop. I was exceedingly interested in the subject matter, and equally so in the characters. I was very much impressed by Mr. Wolfe's handling of the interplay of character with the boom conditions in the town.

I like the form of the play and in almost every scene my

attention was held more and more rigidly up to the climax. I was tremendously impressed by the dramatic quality of these climaxes—quite free as they were from artificiality and banality. I cannot praise the play too highly—and yet I suppose that the minor criticisms which I have to offer might be of more assistance to Mr. Wolfe than commendation.

Of the various scenes making up the play, none of which could be spared, some could be cut to advantage in my opinion. The political conversations were unnecessarily long. They had nothing to offer except as examples of the point of view of such men, and in my opinion should be cut down to the minimum amount necessary to carry their characters. I was restless and bored once I had "got the numbers" of the governor and his group, and their relations to conditions in the town. I would not cut out entirely either the before-the-election or the after-the-election scenes, because of differences in attitude which were brought out by political victory, but I would cut the length of their conversations in relation to generalities, and perhaps give each of them a definite chance to air his personal opinion on the specific case of the "fired" professor.

In the library scene Mrs. Rutledge's conversation could also be cut. The impression of futile efforts at culture could and should be given I think more casually and indirectly, and less by a direct monologue from her to her listening husband. I regret that we did not get a glimpse of the judge's and Mrs. Rutledge's opinion of Lee, his life, and friends, and the younger generation. This would be of more compelling interest than a monologue about futile drama club activities—and would allow more interplay and reaction between husband and wife—on a subject of intense common interest to both of them—and to us.

In the very last scene Judge Rutledge's vague and wandering philosophies could be quite eliminated. In my opinion the last scene would be much more powerful if when he asked to be alone (as he did) and then sat there by the side of the mulatto, he quietly listened, eagerly and intensely, to what Johnson had to say;—his attitude that now at last he was going to understand.

I should drop the final curtain when Johnson sees the irony of having spent his life fighting desperately things outside of himself, only at the moment of his death to discover that he himself was a hopeless misfit—neither white nor black.

My only other suggestion is as to the name. "Welcome to Our City" suggests to me something lightweight—with no pretense at reality or earnestness of purpose. Such a suggestion is I think unfortunate. I suggest a number of names—none of which are good—but which to me carry an idea more along the line of the purpose of the play. The name should suggest that it is a play about a place—and if possible that the play is in the South and distinctly American. My suggestions are

"Carolina, U.S.A." or
"Local Patriotism" or
"The Boom Town" or
"The New South."

I will just say again that the play is one of the best I have ever seen at the Shop. Perhaps even the very best.

CRITIQUE NUMBER TWO:

As this play opened, with its scene so reminiscent of [Molnar's] *Liliom* yet nevertheless intriguing, I anticipated some novel treatment of the comedy of manners. But instead of manners and customs being the background for the activity of individuals, they became the plot itself. That idea of making the life of a city the plot of a play seems to me not only intensely interesting, but almost limitless in its possibilities. To avoid a merely kaleidoscopic picture and gain instead a continuity of action through such diversified interests, must tax the author's power in handling plot. Accustomed, too, as we are to following the fate of individuals, or at the most groups of individuals, we find that we must readjust our ideas of plot structures. I am inclined to think that even the vaudeville buffoonery of the "bed-room scene" was justified as it became the author's penetrating comment on the insincerity of politicians.

The characterization was powerful and amazingly accurate. The unflinching courage with which the South's problem was faced gives one hope for its ultimate solution. The telling artistry in the presentation and the effective stage management, particularly in the passing by of the workmen, made the performance Saturday night in many ways the most impressive I have seen this year, but I am convinced that the play's real distinction is in the tremendous scope of its plan. It seems to me that Mr. Wolfe is doing for the drama what Tolstoi did for the novel.